The Beginning Guide to
Microsoft PowerPoint 2010
Microsoft Office Specialist Exam 77-883 Study Guide

another
Computer
Mama
Guide

© 2012 Comma Productions, LLC

Beginning Guide to Microsoft PowerPoint 2010

© 2012 Comma Productions, LLC
9090 Chilson Road
Brighton, MI 48116
978-0-9800656-4-0

Trademark and Copyright

Limit of Liability/Disclaimer of Warranty:

another
Computer Mama
Guide

Beginning Guide to Microsoft PowerPoint 2010

Microsoft Office Specialist Certification

What is the Microsoft Office Specialist Certification?

The Microsoft Office Specialist certification validates through the use of exams that you have obtained specific skill sets within the applicable Microsoft Office programs and other Microsoft programs included in the Microsoft Office Specialist Program. The candidate can choose which exam(s) they want to take according to which skills they want to validate.

CertiPort is the premier provider for validating technology skills.

The **Microsoft Office Specialist** tests are offered at authorized testing centers.

For more information on the MOS exam topics or to find a testing center near you please contact: **www.certiport.com**

What is the Microsoft Office Specialist Certification Program?

The **Microsoft Office Specialist (MOS) Certification Program** enables candidates to show that they have something exceptional to offer – proven expertise in Microsoft Office programs. Recognized by businesses and schools around the world, millions of certifications have been obtained in over 100 different countries. The **Microsoft Office Specialist (MOS) Certification Program** is the only Microsoft-approved certification program of its kind.

The Microsoft Office Specialist Certification Series

Core Certification: Pass any 1 test:
Word 2010 Core: Exam 77-881
Excel® 2010 Core: Exam 77-882
PowerPoint® 2010: Exam 77-883
Access® 2010: Exam 77-885
Outlook® 2010: Exam 77-884

Expert Certification: Pass either test:
Word 2010 Expert: Exam 77-887
Excel® 2010 Expert: Exam 77-888

Master: Pass 3 required and 1 elective test:
Required
Word 2010 Expert: Exam 77-887
Excel® 2010 Expert: Exam 77-888
PowerPoint® 2010: Exam 77-883

Elective
Access® 2010: Exam 77-885 or
Outlook® 2010: Exam 77-884

⌒ The Benefits of Certification

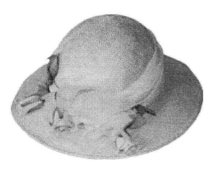

For More Information:
www.certiport.com
www.microsoft.com

Why Get Certified?

For employers, the certification provides skill-verification tools that not only help assess a person's skills in using Microsoft Office programs but also the ability to quickly complete on-the-job tasks across multiple programs in the Microsoft Office system. (http://www.microsoft.com/learning/en/us/certification/mos.aspx). Certification proves a certain level of advanced competency with the programs in question. Employers don't have to wonder if the skills stated on the resume are honest and without exaggeration. This can lead to further employment opportunities and increased pay.

A person holding Microsoft Office Certification shows not just a level of skill, but an ability to quickly complete tasks, due to familiarity with the program and it's many time-saving features. The hard work that goes into learning Microsoft Office programs to the level of proficiency necessary for successful completion of the Certification Exams also indicates a desire on behalf of the student to learn and succeed.

The Benefits: Earn More, Find Jobs Quicker

Research indicates that employees with Microsoft Certification earn more and find jobs quicker than those employees without certification. Furthermore, employees with certification report a greater feeling of confidence. These things translate into greater job satisfaction. (http://www.microsoft.com/learning/en/us/certification/mos.aspx)

Research also shows that individuals with certification make up to 12% more than those without certification. In addition, 82% of Microsoft Office Specialists report a salary increase after receiving certification. Managers like the skills proven and the ability demonstrated by those with Microsoft Office Certifications.
http://www.certiport.com/Portal/desktopdefault.aspx?page=common/pagelibrary/mos2003.html

About Our Certification Program

Books in this Series:
Beginning Guide to
Microsoft® PowerPoint 2010

Advanced Guide to
Microsoft® PowerPoint 2010

Microsoft Office Specialist (MOS) Certification for PowerPoint 2010

Overview: Our Microsoft Office Specialist certification program for PowerPoint 2010 has two levels of mastery: Beginning and Advanced. These guides cover all of the exam objectives for the PowerPoint certification exam.

Our Approach: In designing these Guides, we found that it made more sense to write the lessons based on the Ribbons and Tasks. For example, the Beginning Guide to Microsoft PowerPoint 2010 shows all of the Picture Tools. The beginning of each lesson provides an overview of the Ribbons and Tasks covered.

The Beginning Guide to Microsoft PowerPoint 2010 demonstrates the following Ribbons: Home, Insert, Design, Picture Tools: Format, Smart Art Tools: Design, Smart Art Tools: Format, and View. Also, basic Backstage commands are covered. The lessons focus on basic content and design commands, as well as working with pictures and graphics.

The Advanced Guide to Microsoft PowerPoint 2010 demonstrates the following Ribbons: Table Tools: Layout, Table Tools: Design, Chart Tools: Layout, Chart Tools: Design, Chart Tools: Format, Slide Master, Transitions, Animations, Video Tools: Format, Video Tools: Playback, Slide Show, Review, and Notes Master. Advanced Backstage commands and options are covered. The activities focus on adding animations and multimedia to slide shows, as well as preparing to present the slide show.

Course Prerequisites: Students who enroll in the Microsoft Office Specialist (MOS) program should have basic computer skills, including how to turn on the computer, how to use an Internet browser, and how to select commands from a menu. Students show know how to save files and send attachments by email as well.

Microsoft PowerPoint 2010 Study Guide: Beginning
Microsoft Office Specialist (MOS): Exam 77-883 for PowerPoint 2010

Microsoft PowerPoint 2010 Study Guide: Beginning
Microsoft Office Specialist (MOS): Exam 77-883 for PowerPoint 2010

About the Authors

Elizabeth Ann Nofs

Elizabeth is the Computer Mama. She developed the teaching methodology in the Complete Computer Guide series using breakthrough research in gender balanced training. Elizabeth has taught several thousand men and women from government, manufacturing, small business, and education in both online and hands-on classrooms.

She is the author of the Complete Computer Guides as well as a Microsoft Certified Office Specialist. She earned a BA in Biology from the University of Michigan.

Alex Sergay, Senior Instructional Designer

For more than 20 years, Alex has made complex technology easy to understand. Alex has developed instructional multimedia software for educational websites including the Sounds of English, a linguistics-training tool that earned a ComputerWorld/Smithsonian Laureate.

Alex earned his Masters of Educational Technology from the University of Michigan, Ann Arbor.

Clair Dickson, Student Services

Clair works with adult learners in online, face-to-face and hybrid classroom settings. She is considered "highly qualified" to teach introductory computers, including Microsoft Office.

Clair has a Graduate Certificate in Educational Media and Technology, an program that explored ways to infuse technology into the learning experience so that learning is interactive. She has earned Microsoft Office 2007 Master Certification. She also holds a BS in Secondary English Education from Eastern Michigan University.

Leo Michael Nofs, Technical Writing and Quality Control

Leo is a Microsoft Certified Professional and an Access database designer. He uses his exemplary attention to detail for copy editing the computer instructions for accuracy and clarity.

Traci Nofs, Photography and Photo Editing

Traci has been photographing children and nature since 2000. She works freelance out of her home, including weddings, engagements, and particularly children's photography. She has further enhanced her photos by use of image manipulation, focusing on light and color.

M. Jeanette McCrickard, Office Manager

Jeanette has years of experience as an office manager, including the increasing use of computer-related tasks. Her excellent attention to detail has lead her to work as an Access database administrator and a copy editor.

All of my books

are dedicated to

Fr. Paul Cummings

who taught me

computers.

Love, eBeth

How To Use This Guide
Microsoft Office Specialist Certification Training

The Comma Method

Observation is a perceptual strategy that asks: why am I doing this and which tools would be most effective? Each lesson begins with a discussion of the purpose and the objectives.

Orientation helps students start at the right place. The screen shots in the *Complete Compute Guides* show the entire window as well as a close up of the particular button or command.

Notation There are "breadcrumbs" above each screen image. Like Hansel and Gretel, the breadcrumbs show the pathway to a button or option. Our notation uses the following convention:
Ribbon->Group->Button->Options

Menu Maps

The Comma Method recognizes that there is a difference in how men and women navigate the menus. Men typically have the ability to see the map first. This method of acquiring knowledge is called *Breadth-first.* [1] Women tend to work with the details first. They learn several commands, such as copy, cut, and paste, then they put those concepts under the label, "edit." This method of learning is called *Depth-first.*

The Comma Method uses menu mapping to assist men and women to see both the Breadth and the Depth. An example of the menu map is can be seen here.

[1] Ford, Nigel, Sherry Chen, Matching/mismatching revisited: An Empirical Study of Learning and Teaching Styles. British Journal of Educational Technology v.32 no1 (Jan. 2001)

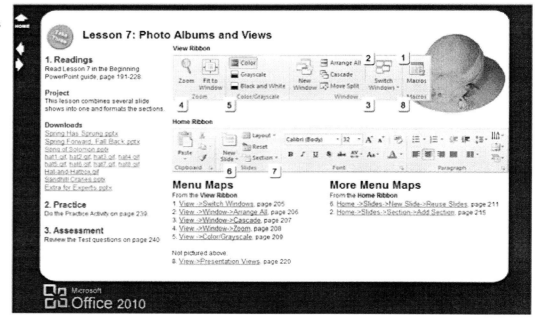

Picture Tools-> Format->Adjust

PowerPoint 2010: Getting Started

Welcome!

Course Objectives

Students will be able to:

1. Log in to the online course

2. Navigate the outline and lessons

3. Take quizzes online

4. Submit assignments online

5. Participate in the Forums and Chat

HOME

Welcome

This course presents a practical, hands-on approach to computers. The lessons are based on what you see on the screen, what you can do with the options, and what works on the job. The goal is to enable you to use Microsoft Windows and Office 2010 effectively, even creatively.

Use this *Guide* as part of your professional development plan to prepare for the new Microsoft Business Certification (Microsoft Office Specialist (MOS) or as a reference book to solve problems as they come up.

This introduction provides information on:
• Navigation
• Practice
• Sample Documents
• Assessments

Log into the course

This online course requires a User Name and Password. You probably received an email with your username and password when you enrolled.

Try This: Login
Go to the website for your course.
1. Click on the (Login) link.
2. You will be prompted for your Username and Password.

What If This Doesn't Work?
First, look at the keyboard and make sure the Caps Lock is off (no light.) Passwords need both upper and lower case letters.

Second, check the spelling. Your user name may not be exactly the same as your email address.

Third, you can click on the Live Chat and get immediate assistance.

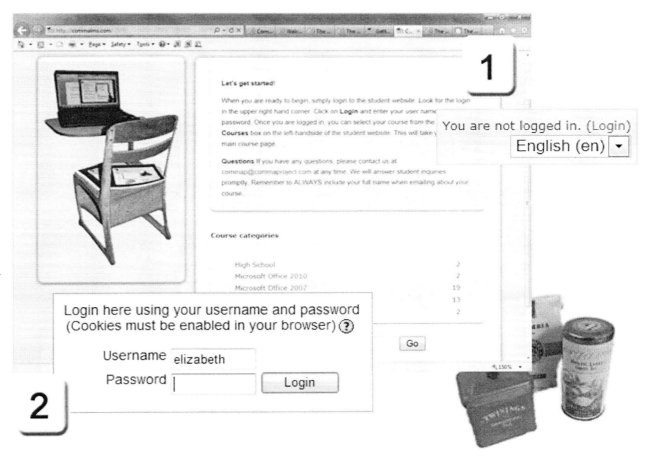

The Topic Outline

When you log into your course, you should see the **Topic Outline**. The Topic Outline is a course syllabus: it lists your lessons, practice and quizzes.

Each Level has Lessons and Assessments. The lesson links are short discussions that demonstrate the options on a particular Ribbon. The lessons links may also list the page number where these pages can be found in the print version of the computer guides.

Many students prefer to read the lessons on a second monitor or in print, rather than switch from the lesson screens to Microsoft Office to practice the options.

Memo to Self: It's OK if your computer does not match exactly. The important part is learning the steps. Please contact your facilitator if you have any questions

My Course ->Topic Outline

Lesson Links

When you click on a hyperlink to read a lesson, a new window will open.

What Do You See? On the left side of each screen you should see the white navigation arrows: Next, Previous, and Home

What Else Do You See? When you are done with a lesson, you can close the browser window. Go to the upper right corner of the lesson window and click on the X to Exit.

The Topic Outline should be there, the window was left open behind the lesson screen.

My Course ->Topic Outline ->Lesson

Download the Samples

Each Level may have many sample files (or none), depending on which course you are taking. When there are downloads, there will be instructions on how to download and save the sample files to your computer.

What Do You See? Your computer may NOT MATCH the pictures that you see in the books or online. The screen shots may be different depending on which version of Windows you are using, or even which Internet Browser you prefer.

Memo to Self: It's OK if your computer does not match exactly. The important part is learning the steps. Please contact your facilitator if you have any questions

My Course ->Topic Outline -> Downloads

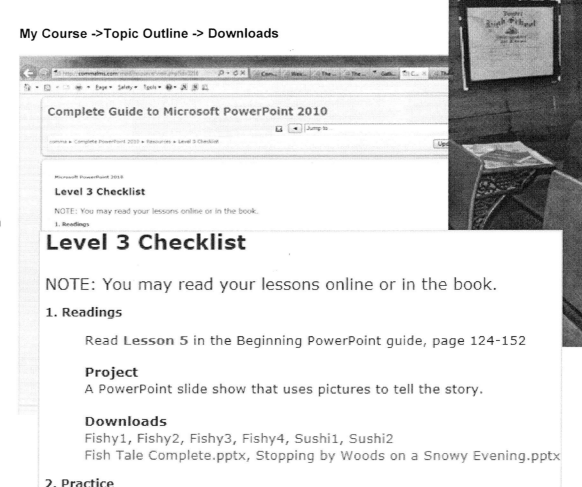

Complete Guide to Microsoft PowerPoint 2010

Level 3 Checklist

NOTE: You may read your lessons online or in the book.

1. Readings

Level 3 Checklist

NOTE: You may read your lessons online or in the book.

1. Readings

Read **Lesson 5** in the Beginning PowerPoint guide, page 124-152

Project
A PowerPoint slide show that uses pictures to tell the story.

Downloads
Fishy1, Fishy2, Fishy3, Fishy4, Sushi1, Sushi2
Fish Tale Complete.pptx, Stopping by Woods on a Snowy Evening.pptx

2. Practice

Take a Quiz Online

After you review the materials online or with the *Guides*, you can log into the course online and take a **Quiz**. This is an open book quiz. You are allowed to look up the answers in your notes, online, or in the computer *Guides*.

Review the Quiz Buttons
Submit: This button posts your answer for the current question.

Save without submitting: This button saves your answers. You can leave the quiz and finish it later.

> Save without submitting

Submit page: This button sends your answers to all questions on the page.

Submit all and finish: Use this button to finish the quiz and post your results online.

> Submit all and finish

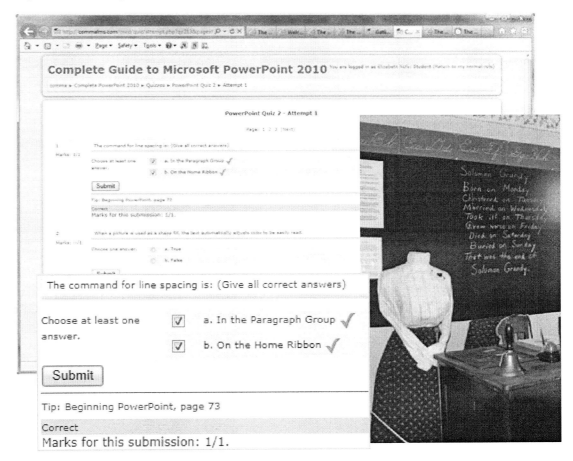

The command for line spacing is: (Give all correct answers)

Choose at least one answer.
☑ a. In the Paragraph Group ✓
☑ b. On the Home Ribbon ✓

Submit

Tip: Beginning PowerPoint, page 73

Correct
Marks for this submission: 1/1.

Submit Your Work

Many online courses ask you to upload a document or a spreadsheet. Here are the steps.

Try This: Upload a file
1. Go to the Topic Outline.
Click on Submit...

What Do You See? The instructions should be repeated on the screen.

2. Click on **Browse** to select the file you want to upload. Navigate to your file, then click **Open**. The path and file name will appear in the upload box.

3. Click **Upload this file** to submit the file to your instructor.

NOTICE: There may be a **maximum size** to this assignment. Some examples, say richly illustrated PowerPoint slide shows, may be too big. If so, please contact your instructor.

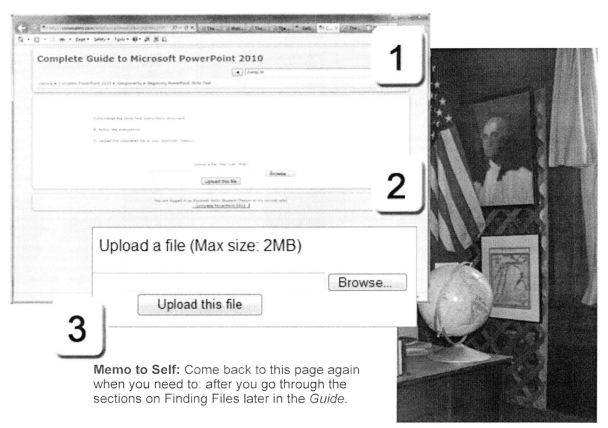

Memo to Self: Come back to this page again when you need to: after you go through the sections on Finding Files later in the *Guide*.

Use the Forums

In an online class, a **Forum** is similar to raising your hand and asking a question. When you post a question to a Forum anyone can reply with a suggestion or comment. Some of the answers are very creative and useful.

Your instructor may also post an explanation or offer additional links.

Edit | Delete | Reply

Live Chats

Many instructors keep Office Hours. Chat allows you to type questions online and get an answer immediately from your instructor when your instructor is in the office.

Don't Explain and Don't Complain:
Please keep your posts professional and on topic!

My Course ->Topic Outline -> Activities

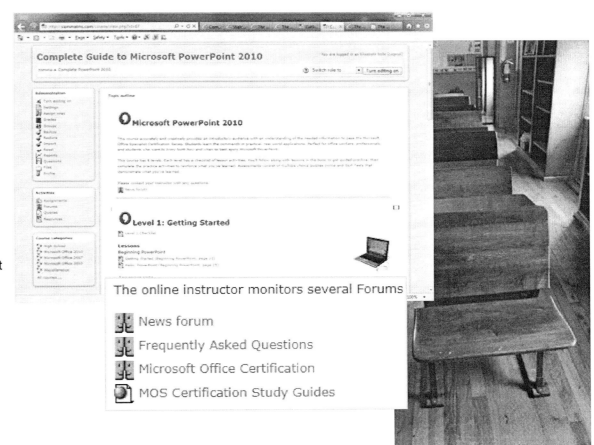

The online instructor monitors several Forums

News forum

Frequently Asked Questions

Microsoft Office Certification

MOS Certification Study Guides

Practice

This *Guide* offers additional reference materials and practice certification tests. You can use the multiple choice quizzes and skill tests to practice if you wish. When you are ready, please log into the course and do the assessments online.

The Microsoft certification tests are timed: you have to perform the process steps very quickly and efficiently in order to pass.

That takes practice!

More practice

If you have a question about a document or file you are working on you are always welcome to email a copy of your work to your instructor as an attachment.

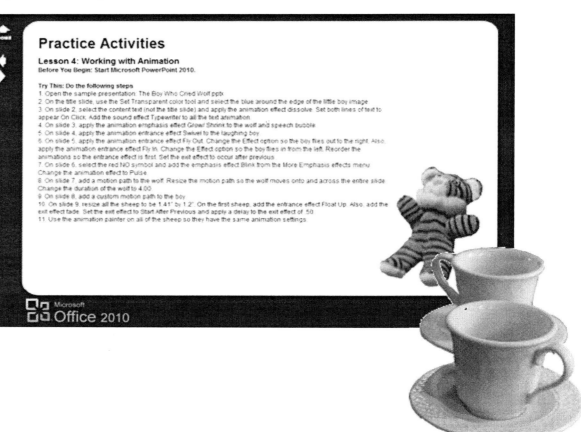

Microsoft Business Certification

The course prepares you to pass the **Microsoft Office Specialist (MOS)** exams. This credential recognizes the business skills needed to get the most out of Microsoft Office 2010.

Microsoft Certification Exams are available through authorized testing centers. They are not included as part of the certification training program in the same way that taking the Bar Exam is not included with getting a degree in Law from a college or university.

More Information Online.
Certiport provides the official Microsoft certification tests. You can download the Microsoft certification topics and study guides. Here is their address: www.certiport.com

Please Note: *Comma Productions, LLC. is independent from Microsoft Corporation, and not affiliated with Microsoft in any manner. While the Complete Computer Guides may be used in assisting individuals to prepare for a Microsoft Business Certification exam, Microsoft, its designated program administrator, and Comma Productions, LLC. do not warrant that use of these Complete Computer Guides will ensure passing a Microsoft Business Certification exam.*

Can Microsoft Office 2010 Starter be used for Microsoft Office certification training?

Yes and No. The Microsoft Excel 2010 Starter software has all of the features required to practice and prepare for the Microsoft Excel 2010 CORE certification test. The Microsoft Word 2010 Starter software is missing several key features that are part of the Microsoft Office 2010 CORE certification requirements.

Compare the MOS CORE certification topics
The Microsoft Word 2010 Starter:
Word 2010 MOS CORE certification topics (PDF)

The Microsoft Excel 2010 Starter:
EXCEL 2010 MOS CORE certification topics (PDF)

With the Office 2010 Starter evaluation:
Office 2010 Starter evaluation (PDF)

More information on Office Starter software:
View an image of Word 2010 Starter
View an image of Excel 2010 Starter

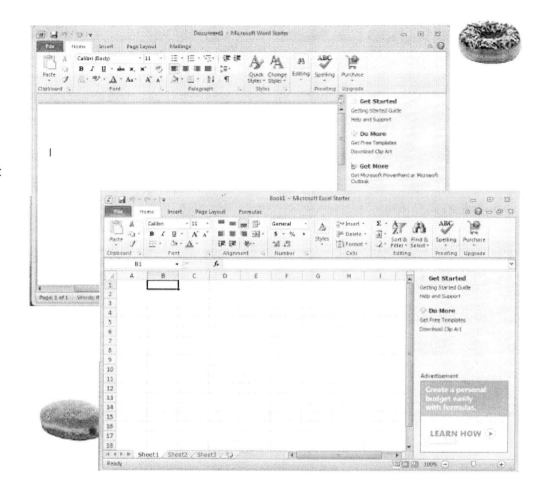

Self-Assessment

Skill Level-Beginning PowerPoint	Mastered	Needs Work	Required for my job
Create presentations from templates			
Add and modify slides			
Organize slides in the slide sorter			
Format Text boxes: borders, effects			
Format bulleted lists			
Apply Quick Styles and Themes			
Apply animation to slides and objects			
Add hyperlinks to the presentation			
Check compatibility and privacy			
Password protect the presentation			

Beginning PowerPoint is recommended if you selected "needs work" on three or more skills.

Skill Level-Advanced PowerPoint	Mastered	Needs Work	Required for my job
Create slides from blank presentations			
Modify the Slide Masters			
Add placeholders			
Add an Action button			
Insert and modify Tables			
Insert and modify SmartArt			
Insert and modify Charts			
Add sound and movies			
Rehearse and package the presentation			
Create and edit speaker handouts			

Advanced PowerPoint is recommended if you selected "needs work" on three or more skills.

Memo to Self:

My Login Information
User Name:

Password:

Website:

My Instructor
Name:

Email:

Office Hours:

PowerPoint 2010: Getting Started

Hello, PowerPoint!

PowerPoint Objectives
In this lesson, you will learn how to:

1. Use the **Home** Ribbon to add a new slide

2. Enter Text on a slide

3. Use the **Font** Group to format the Text: Bold, Italic, Underline, and Color

4. Use the **Font** Group to modify the type face

5. Modify the **Font Size**: Increase and Decrease

6. Find **More Font Options**

7. Use the **Backstage** to Save a file in the pptx file format as well as the legacy ppt file format

© 2011 Comma Productions LLC

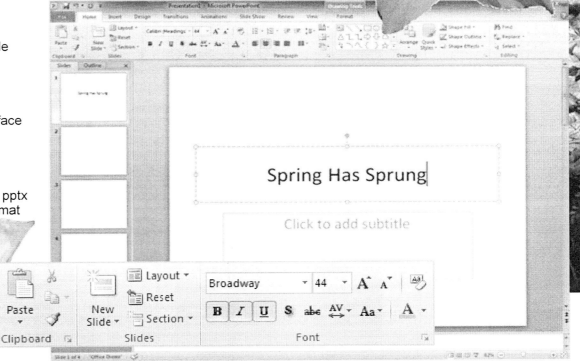

Lesson 2 : Hello, PowerPoint

Home Ribbon

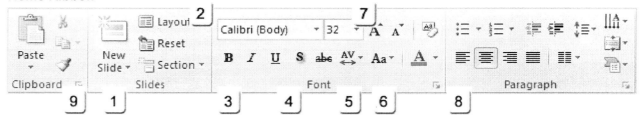

1. Readings

Read Lesson 2 in the PowerPoint guide, page 25-51.

Project

A simple presentation that demonstrates how to edit text on slides.

Downloads

Spring Has Sprung.pptx

2. Practice

Complete the Practice Activity on page 52.

3. Assessment

Review the Test questions on page 52.

Menu Maps

From the **Home Ribbon**.
1. Home ->Slides->New Slide, page 29
2. Home ->Font->Font, page 32
3. Home ->Font->Bold, page 33
4. Home ->Font->Shadow, page 34
5. Home ->Font->Character Spacing, page 34
6. Home ->Font->Change Case, page 36
7. Home ->Font->Size, page 37
8. Home ->Font->More, page 39
9. Home ->Clipboard-> Copy, page 41

More Menu Maps

From the **Backstage**
1. File ->Save, page 46
2. File ->Save As-> PowerPoint 97-2003, page 48
3. File ->Options->Save, page 50

Hello, PowerPoint

PowerPoint is part of the same Microsoft Office 2010 suite as Word, Excel, Access and Outlook. Each program has a purpose: Excel makes spreadsheets, Word edits documents, and PowerPoint makes slide shows. PowerPoint is just as rich as Word or Excel with many advanced options for **pictures, videos, sounds, and animation.** The tools are fun, effective and very creative.

PowerPoint is used by everyone who wants to speak to an audience. A good show can make people look, listen, and learn. Show them why your product or your method is better. That's what PowerPoint is supposed to do: **tell the story.**

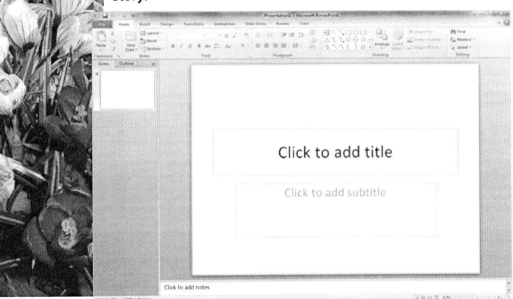

Please Start Microsoft PowerPoint
What do you see at the top of the screen? Is there a Title Bar that says Microsoft PowerPoint? Yes.

Is there a **Home** Ribbon with the Clipboard, Font and Paragraph Groups? Yes.

If your screen looks similar to the example on this page, then you are ready to get started.

Getting Started

Microsoft PowerPoint creates slide shows. The program opens with a new, blank presentation that has one slide.

Our lesson will begin by entering and formatting text on a slide. All of the options will be from the **Home** Ribbon.

Try it: Review the Home Ribbon
The options on the **Home** Ribbon are placed in **Groups** that more or less make sense. The Groups are:
Clipboard
Slides
Font
Paragraph
Drawing
Editing

What Else Do You See? Look in the upper left corner. There are two tabs in the navigation pane: **Slides** and **Outline**.

Keep going...

Microsoft PowerPoint 2010

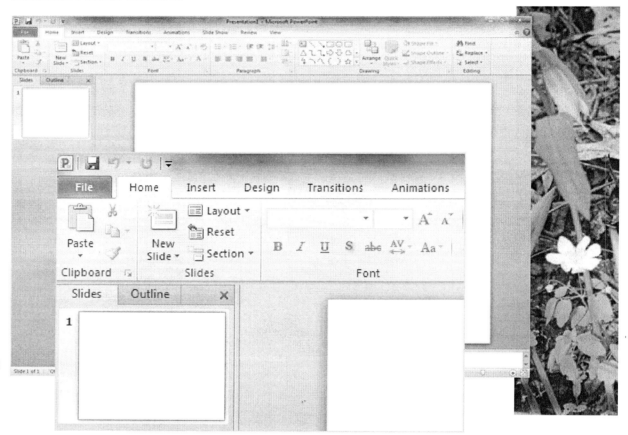

Add a New Slide

Every slide show needs slides. Here are the steps to add a new slide.

1. Try it: Add a New Slide
Go to **Home ->Slides.**
Click on **New Slide.**
Click **New Slide**, again.
Click New Slide, once more.

What Do You See? There should be four slides in the navigation pane on the left.

Keep going...!

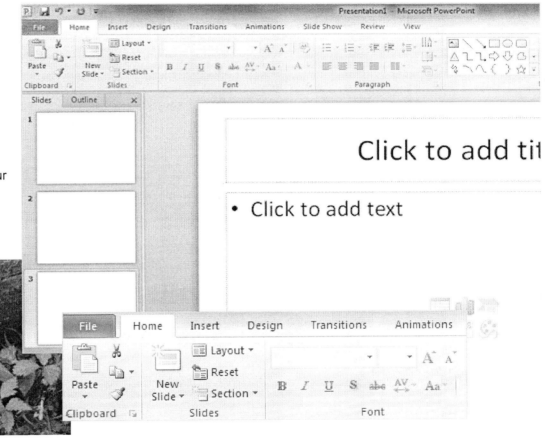

Exam 77-883: Microsoft PowerPoint 2010
2. Creating a Slide Presentation
2.3. Add and remove slides: New Slide

Add Text to a Slide

The first slide, the **Title Slide**, has a different layout than the rest of the slides. The Title slide is like the cover on a book.

The technical term for the Text Box is **Placeholder**. The first example adds text into the placeholder.

Before You Begin: Use the Slide Pane on the left side to select Slide 1.

Try it: Enter Text in a Text Box
Slide 1 is selected. There are two Text Boxes. Click in the top Text Box.
Type: Spring Has Sprung

What Do You See? The Text Box has a dashed line around the Border. There are **handles** in each corner and on the sides.

What Else Do You See? The words in the Title are big (44 pt) and centered.

Keep going..

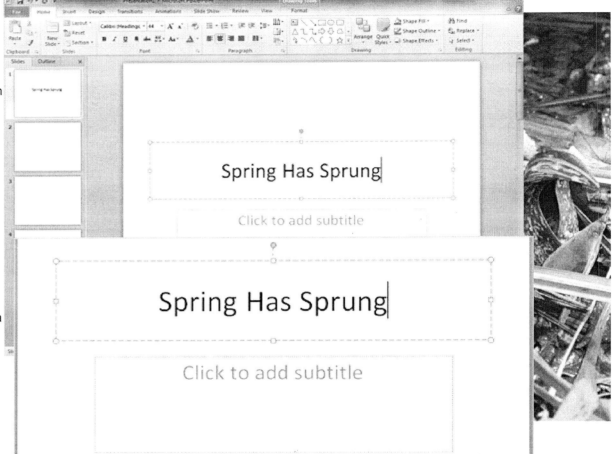

Exam 77-883: Microsoft PowerPoint 2010
2. Creating a Slide Presentation
2.5. Enter and format text: Enter Text in a Text Box

Add Text to Other Slides
Please add the following poem to the slides.
There will be one line of the poem in the top
Text Box, the Title, on each slide.

Try it: Add Text to Other Slides
Select Slide 2.
Type: Spring Has Sprung

Select Slide 3.
Type: The Grass Has Riz

Select Slide 4.
Type: I Wonder Where the Flowers Iz

What Do You see? Microsoft PowerPoint,
like Word, checks your spelling as you type.
This poem by Ogden Nash is spelled the way
the writer wanted it, but the funny words do
not match ones that are in the dictionary.

Keep going...

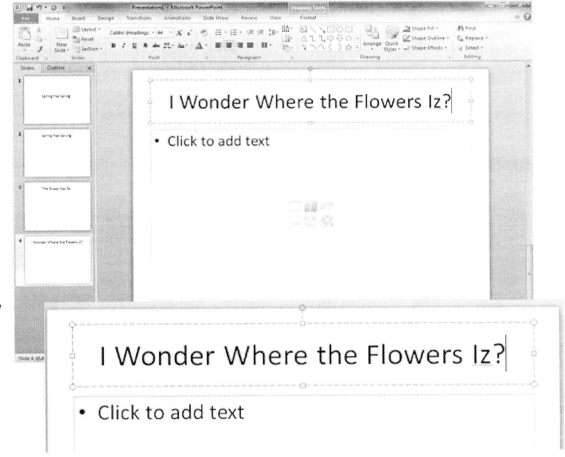

Exam 77-883: Microsoft PowerPoint 2010
2. Creating a Slide Presentation
2.5. Enter and format text: Enter Text in a Text Box

Format the Font

The **Home** Ribbon has a rich set of options for formatting the Text. The **Font** Group includes Font (type face), Size, Style, (Bold, Italic, Underline, Shadow), Character Spacing and Color. Let's look at the options.

2. Try it: Format the Text

Go to Slide 4.
Double click the word Flowers to select it.
Go to **Home->Font->Font**.
Select **Broadway** from the list of Fonts.

What Do You See? Microsoft PowerPoint offers a **Live Preview** as you run the mouse over the Fonts in the list.

Memo to Self: Should you use plain or fancy Fonts? The decorative type faces are fun and each one invokes a different feeling. Fancy Fonts work best on Titles. Smaller text is easier to read if it is san serif (plain, no curly cues) such as Arial, Helvetica and Tahoma.

Keep going...

Exam 77-883: Microsoft PowerPoint 2010
2. Creating a Slide Presentation
2.5. Enter and format text: Change Text Format

Format the Text

You can emphasize key words or phrases in your presentation by formatting the text bold or with a different color.

3. Try it: Format the Text
Go to Slide 4.
Double click the word Flowers to select it.
Go to **Home->Font.**
Click on B for **Bold.**
Click on I for **Italic.**
Click on U for **Underline.**

Try This, Too: Format the Color
The word Flowers is selected.
Go to **Home->Font->Color.**
Select a Standard Color: Light Green

What Do You See? Each of the Font Styles that you applied are highlighted: Bold, Italic, Underline and Light Green.

Keep going...

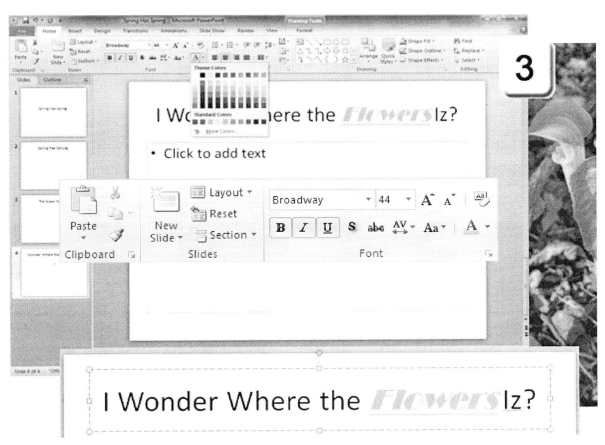

Exam 77-883: Microsoft PowerPoint 2010
2. Creating a Slide Presentation
2.5. Enter and format text: Change Text Format (Bold, Italic, Underline, Color)

Take Two

Format the Font Shadow

Adding a **Shadow** makes the type easier to read on the screen. Here are the steps:

4. Try This, Too: Format the Shadow
Double click the word Flowers to select it.
Go to **Home->Font.**
Click on S for **Shadow.**

So far, so good. Keep going...

Home ->Font->Shadow

4

Exam 77-883: Microsoft PowerPoint 2010
2. Creating a Slide Presentation
2.5. Enter and format text: Format Text Shadow

Change the Character Spacing

Character Spacing is the amount of white space between the letters. In typography, this is called kerning. (The Computer Mama sez: I always pictured kernels of corn on the cob.)

5. Try it: Format the Character Spacing
Select: Flowers.
Go to **Home ->Font->Character Spacing.**
Select: **Very Tight.**

What Do You See? The options include:
Very Tight
Tight
Normal
Loose
Very Loose
More Spacing

Keep going...

Memo to Self: Advertising seems to cycle through Tight (less white space between the characters) and Loose (more white space). If you choose **Very Tight**, look at your text and make sure it is "TNT: Tight, Not Touching."

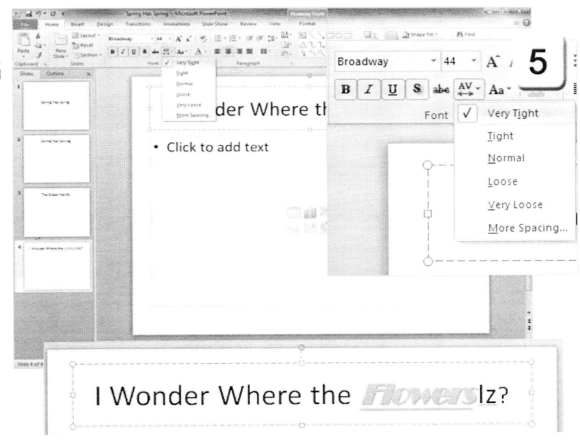

Exam 77-883: Microsoft PowerPoint 2010
2. Creating a Slide Presentation
2.5. Enter and format text: Change Character Spacing

Change Text Case

Case is a technical term for how the text is capitalized.

6. Try This, Too: More Size Options
Select: Flowers.
Go to **Home ->Font->Change Case.**
Select: UPPERCASE.

What Do You See? The options include:
Sentence case: The first word is capitalized.
lowercase
UPPERCASE
Capitalize Each Word
tOGGLE cASE

What Else Do You See? Changing the formatting may make the text wrap (continue) on the second line. The size of the Text Box also increased.

Keep going...

Home ->Font->Change Case

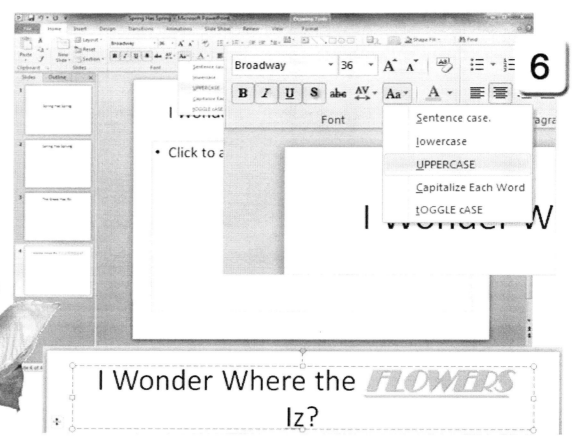

Exam 77-883: Microsoft PowerPoint 2010
2. Creating a Slide Presentation
2.5. Enter and format text: Change Case

Format the Text Size

There are several options for editing the **Text Size**. The first example will format all of the words in the Text Box.

7. Try it: Format the Text Size
Select: I Wonder Where the FLOWERS Iz?
Go to **Home ->Font->Size**.
Select: 36

What Do You See? The text is centered in the Text Box. All of the words fit on one line and it is easier to read.

Keep going...

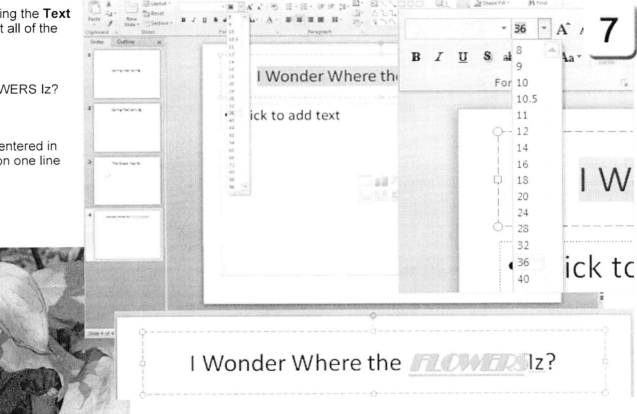

Exam 77-883: Microsoft PowerPoint 2010
2. Creating a Slide Presentation
2.5. Enter and format text: Format Text Size

Increase the Size

Say you wanted to format one word bigger so that it stands out. Here are the steps.

Try it: Increase the Text Size
Select: FLOWERS
Go to **Home ->Font->Increase Font Size.**
Click **Increase Font Size** a couple of times until the text is 54 points.

Keep going...

Memo to Self: How big or small should the Font be? The rule of thumb is nothing smaller than 18 point. It is a good idea to preview your slide show in a darkened room and read the words from 10 feet away. Can you see it?

How big: how big is your idea? <grin>

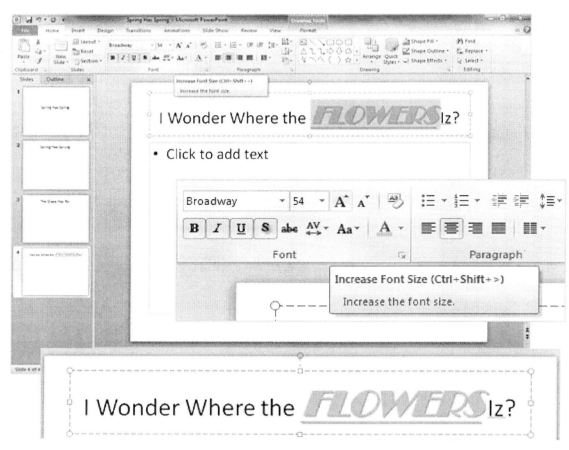

Exam 77-883: Microsoft PowerPoint 2010
2. Creating a Slide Presentation
2.5. Enter and format text: Format Text Size

Find More Font Options

All of the options shown on the Home Ribbon in the **Font** Group are also available when you click on **More**. More is the small arrow on the bottom-right corner of any Group.

8. Try it: Find More Font Options
Select: Flowers
Go to **Home ->Font->More**.

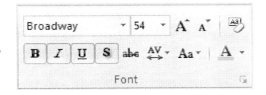

Keep going, please...

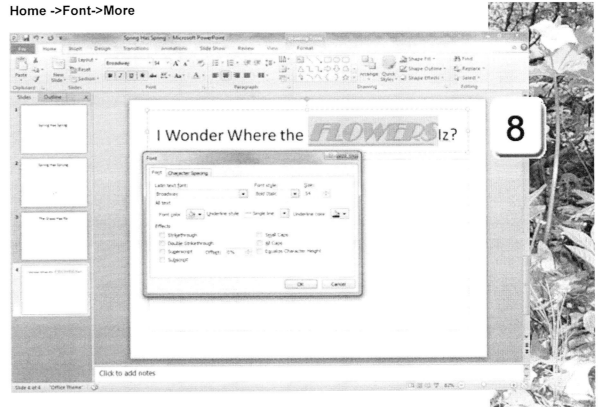

Exam 77-883: Microsoft PowerPoint 2010
2. Creating a Slide Presentation
2.5. Enter and format text: More Font Options

More Font Options

What Do You See: There are two tabs in the **Font** dialogue box: **Font** and **Character Spacing**. The Font tab summarizes the formatting that was applied with the buttons on the **Home** Ribbon:
Latin Text Font: Broadway
Font style: Bold Italic
Size: 54
Color: Light Green

What Else Do You See? There are more **Effects** than shown in the Font Group.
The Effects include:
Strikethrough
Double Strike Through
Superscript
Subscript
Small Caps
All Caps
Equalize Character Height

Click **OK** to close this dialogue box.

Home ->Font->More

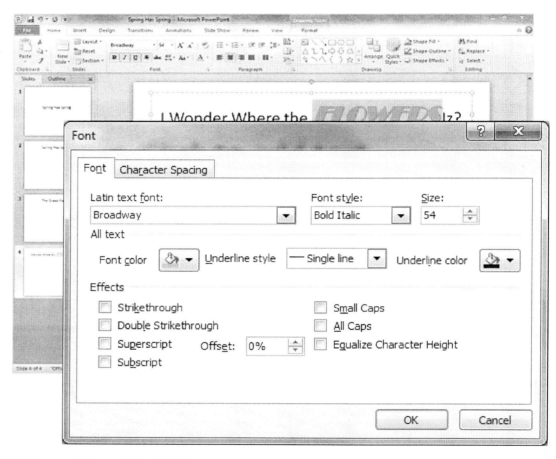

Exam 77-883: Microsoft PowerPoint 2010
2. Creating a Slide Presentation
2.5. Enter and format text: More Font Options

Review the Clipboard Group

The Home Ribbon includes one of the oldest programs ever invented for the computer: the Clipboard. This Group is the Edit commands that were designed in the early 1960's: Cut. Copy, Paste and the Format Painter.

9. Try This: Copy the Text
Select: FLOWERS
Go to **Home ->Clipboard-> Copy.**

Keep going...there's more, of course.

Exam 77-883: Microsoft PowerPoint 2010
2. Creating a Slide Presentation
2.5. Enter and format text: Copy and Paste

Paste and Paste Options
Try This, Too: Paste the Copied Text
Click in the bottom Text Box.
Go to **Home ->Clipboard-> Paste.**

What Do You See? The text that you copied was big, bold and green. The text that was pasted kept most of the same formatting.

Better Look Again: The pasted text is smaller than the copied text. The default size for the Title is 44 points. The default size for the Text in the bottom Text Box is 32 points.

What Else Do You See? There should be a little **Format Painter** next to the pasted text. The options from left to right are:
Use Destination Theme
Keep Source Formatting
Picture
Keep Text Only

The first example shows: **Use Destination Theme.**
The second example shows: **Keep Text Only.**

Keep going..

Home ->Clipboard-> Paste

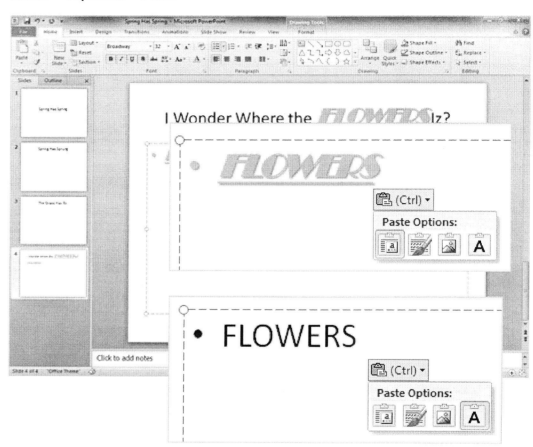

Exam 77-883: Microsoft PowerPoint 2010
2. Creating a Slide Presentation
2.5. Enter and format text: Use the Paste Options

More Paste Options

The **Paste** option on the Home Ribbon is a good example of the new way that Microsoft Office 2007 and 2010 use buttons. The buttons now have two places to click: Top and Bottom.

The Top click is a simple, one step action that does the default command. The Bottom click gives you more options.

Try it: Review the Paste Options
Go to the Title Box.
Select: FLOWERS
Go to **Home ->Clipboard-> Copy.**
Click in the Text Box on the bottom.
Go to **Home ->Clipboard-> Paste.**

What Do You See? If you click on the bottom part of the Paste button, you will see the same **Paste Options** that you saw earlier.

OK, you can click off. Just a little more discussion on Paste...

Home ->Clipboard-> Paste

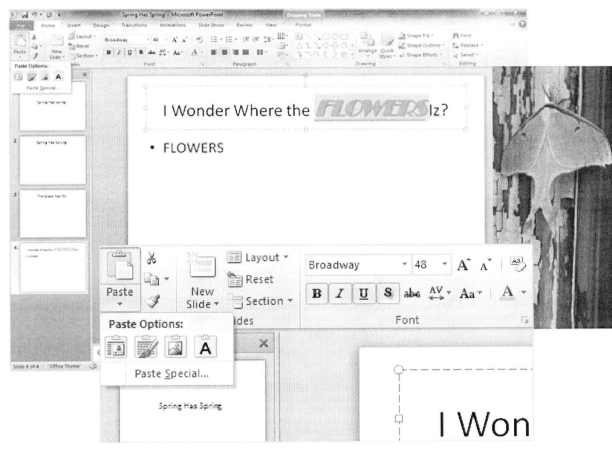

Exam 77-883: Microsoft PowerPoint 2010
2. Creating a Slide Presentation
2.5. Enter and format text: Use the Paste Options

Use The Format Painter

Say you wanted to copy the formatting from the word FLOWERS and apply it to another slide. There is another way to use the Format Painter. Here are the steps.

1. Try it: Select the Formatted Text
1. Select: FLOWERS.

2. Try it: Select the Format Painter
Go to **Home ->Clipboard.**
Click on the **Format Painter.**

What Do You See? Your mouse should have a Format Painter. Whatever you "brush" with the Format Painter will be big, bold, underlined and green.

3. Try it: Use the Format Painter
Go to Slide 3.
Click on: Grass.

The new text should be formatted the same as the text you highlighted initially.

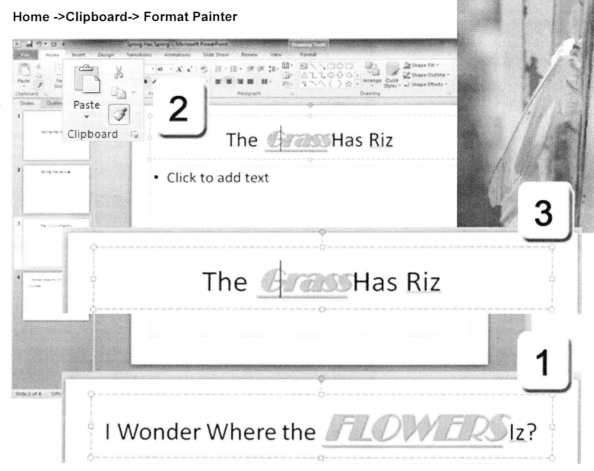

Exam 77-883: Microsoft PowerPoint 2010
2. Creating a Slide Presentation
2.5. Enter and format text: Use the Format Painter

Save Your Presentation

This is a good opportunity to **Save** the Spring slide show. This slide show is the first of many Microsoft PowerPoint presentations that will be combined.

Microsoft PowerPoint 2007 and 2010 have a different file format than previous versions of the PowerPoint software. This lesson will also show how to use **Save As** to create a version of your presentation that can be opened in PowerPoint 97-2003.

Keep going...

File ->Save

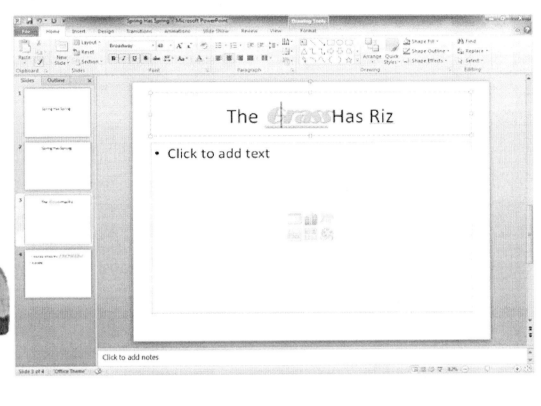

Exam 77-883: Microsoft PowerPoint 2010
7. Preparing Presentations for Delivery
7.1. Save presentations: Save as PPTX

Save Save Save
There are three parts to saving a file:
1. Where are you saving it?
2. What are you calling it?
3. What are you going to do? SAVE!

Here are the steps to save your work and find a folder to keep it in.

Try This: Save a Presentation
Go to **File ->Save.**

What Do You See? This is the Microsoft Office Backstage. The Backstage includes information about the file Permissions, Versions and Properties.
Keep going...

File ->Save

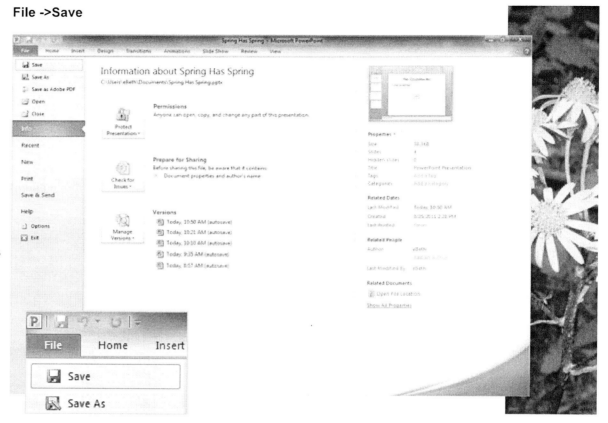

Save or Save As? Both options take you to the same window. You can use **Save As** to create a different version of a document.

Exam 77-883: Microsoft PowerPoint 2010
7. Preparing Presentations for Delivery
7.1. Save presentations: Save as PPTX

Save Options

1. Where Are You Saving It?
By default, Microsoft PowerPoint opens the **Documents** folder on your computer's hard drive as a place to save it. You can use the Documents folder if you wish.

2. What Are You Calling It?
Type the File Name: Spring Has Sprung.

What Do You See? The new file type for Microsoft PowerPoint 2007 and 2010 is the **pptx** format. The pptx format conforms to the new international Open Office standard.

3. What Are You Doing?
Click on **Save.**

When you click **Save**, your slide show will be named, date stamped, and stored in the Documents folder.

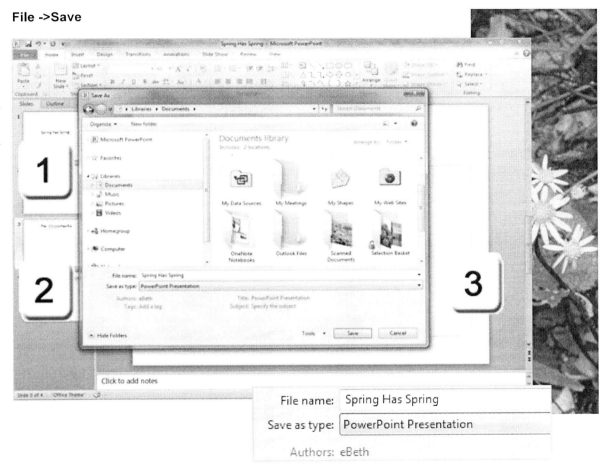

File name:	Spring Has Spring
Save as type:	PowerPoint Presentation
Authors:	eBeth

Exam 77-883: Microsoft PowerPoint 2010
7. Preparing Presentations for Delivery
7.1. Save presentations: Save as PPTX

Save As Office 97-2003

When you save a presentation in Microsoft PowerPoint 2007 or 2010, you should be aware that this is a new file format and that companies with a previous version of Microsoft PowerPoint might not be able to open or edit your work.

Here are the steps you can take to create a copy in PowerPoint 97-2003.

Before You Begin: The Spring Has Sprung.pptx presentation that you saved on the previous page is open.

Try it: Save As Previous Version
Go to **File ->Save A**s.

Keep going...

File ->Save As-> PowerPoint 97-2003

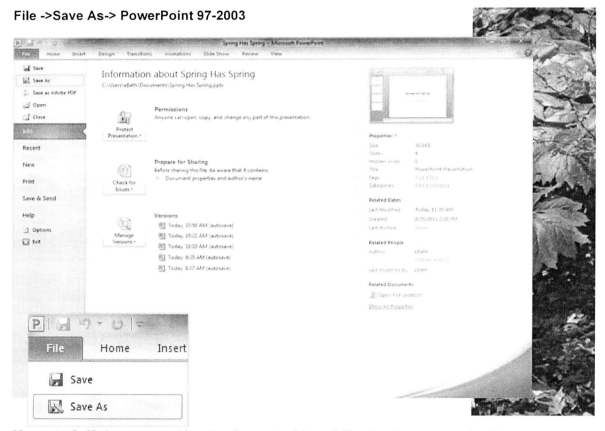

Memo to Self: Are you as old as the Computer Mama? The last time anyone had to consider which version of PowerPoint you should share was in 1997.

Exam 77-883: Microsoft PowerPoint 2010
7. Preparing Presentations for Delivery
7.1. Save presentations: Save as PPT

Save As Office 97-2003

1. Where Are You Saving It?
You can use the Documents folder.

2. What Are You Naming It?
Type the File Name: Spring 97-2003

What Do You See?
The file type is Microsoft PowerPoint 97-2003. It is the **ppt** format. This is the file type that is still used by many businesses, schools and government departments.

3. What Are You Doing?
Click on **Save.**

When you click on **Save,** your presentation will be named, date stamped, and stored in the Documents folder.

File ->Save As-> PowerPoint 97-2003

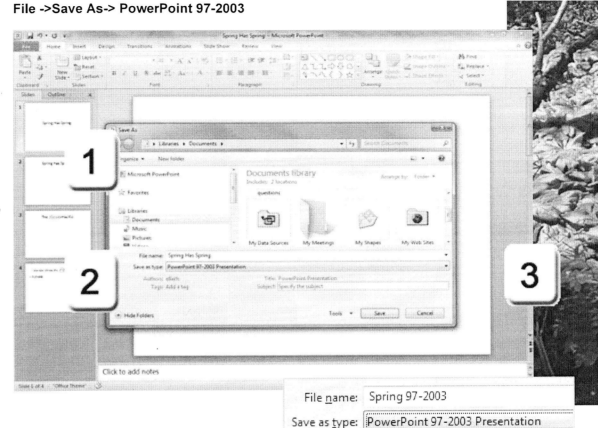

Exam 77-883: Microsoft PowerPoint 2010
7. Preparing Presentations for Delivery
7.1. Save presentations: Save as PPT

Where Did You Save It?

All of the **Microsoft Office** programs save files in the Documents folder. You can change the default location if you wish. This setting is under the **File** menu, with the AutoText options and other tidbits.

Review the Default Location for Saving Your Presentations
Go to **File ->Options**.
Select the category: Save.

What Do You See? You can use the **Browse** button to find and select a different folder to be the default location when you Save a file.

Cancel out of these PowerPoint Options without changing the default file location.

Very good.

File ->Options->Save

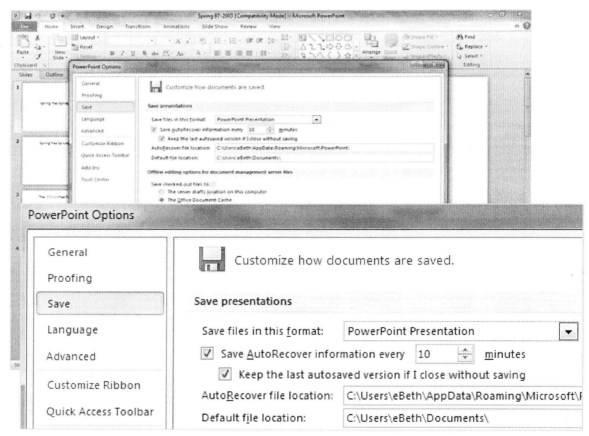

Exam 77-883: Microsoft PowerPoint 2010
1. Managing the PowerPoint Environment
1.4. Configure PowerPoint file options

Lesson Summary

So, Hello Microsoft PowerPoint. This lesson introduced the Font options on the **Home** Ribbon.

The next lesson continues with another Home Ribbon Group: **Paragraph**.

Allez, allez in free.
You get the cookie.

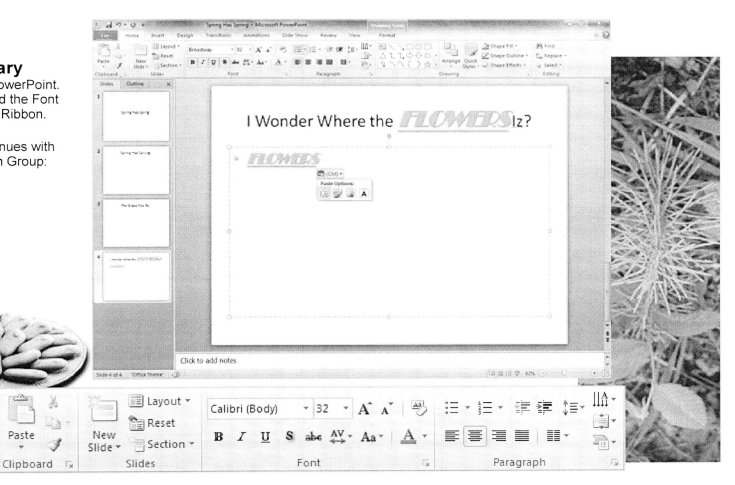

Practice Activities

Lesson 2: Hello, PowerPoint

Before You Begin: Start Microsoft PowerPoint 2010.
You should see a new, blank presentation.

Try This: Do the following steps
1. Start a new blank presentation.
2. Add the Title: Wishes
3. Put your name as the Subtitle.
4. Add 4 more slides. Add the following lines of the poem, with each line on its own slide.
If wishers were horses, then beggars would ride
If turnips were swords, I'd have one by my side
If 'if's and hands were pots and pans,
There would be no need for tinker's hands.
5. Select slide 2 and format the word Wishes in the font Snap (or a bold font of your choice). Change the color to orange the font case to Uppercase.
6. Select slide 3 and format the word If to be bold, italic, and blue.
7. Select slide 4 and format the font size for the words "pots and pans" to be 28 point
8. Select slide 5 and apply double strike-through to the word tinkers. After tinkers, add the word tinsmith's.
9. Copy the word wishes from slide 2 and paste it on slides 3 and 4, so that wishes is formatted the same on all three slides
10. Select the word If on slide 3 and use the format painter tool to format If on slides 2, 4, and 5 the same way.
11. Save the file as Beginning PowerPoint Practice Activity 1

Test Yourself

1. Which of the following is true?
(Give all correct answers.)
a. Word edits documents
b. PowerPoint makes slide shows
c. Excel makes spreadsheets
Tip: Beginning PowerPoint, page 27

2. Which of the following is in the Font Group? (Give all correct answers.)
a. Size
b. Bold
c. Italic
d. Color
Tip: Beginning PowerPoint, page 32

3. The Title slide is formatted the same as the other slides.
a. True
b. False
Tip: Beginning PowerPoint, page 30

4. What commands are found in the clipboard group?
(Give all correct answers)
a. Copy
b. Cut
c. Paste
d. Format Painter
Tip: Beginning PowerPoint, page 41

5. Which is the new file format for PowerPoint 2010?
a. .pptx
b. .ppt
c. .powerpoint
Tip: Beginning PowerPoint, page 47

PowerPoint 2010: Creating a Presentation

P is for Paragraph

Beginning PowerPoint Objectives
In this lesson, you will learn how to:

1. Review the **Spelling** and **Mini Toolbar** options

2. Locate the **Outline** and use the Home Ribbon to add new slides to the Outline View

3. Use the **Paragraph** Group to format the **Bullets**

4. Modify the **Bullets** and choose a different symbol

5. Use the **Paragraph** Group to change the indentation on the bulleted lists

6. Format and modify a **Numbered List**

7. Edit the **Line Spacing** between the paragraphs

8. Modify the Text **Alignment**, **Direction** and position within a Text Box

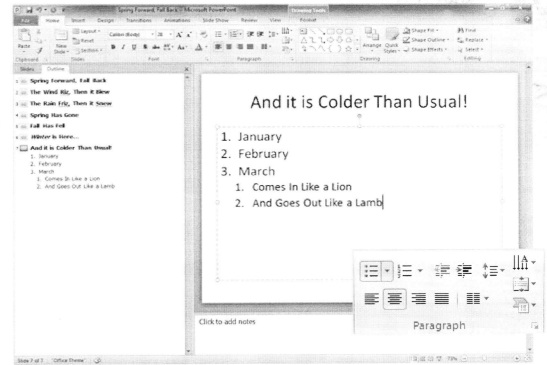

Lesson 3 : P is for Paragraph

1. Readings
Read Lesson 3 in the PowerPoint guide, page 54-80.

Project
A presentation that uses custom text editing with the **Paragraph** options.

Downloads
Spring Forward, Fall Back.pptx

2. Practice
Complete the Practice Activity on page 81.

3. Assessment
Review the Test questions on page 82.

Home Ribbon

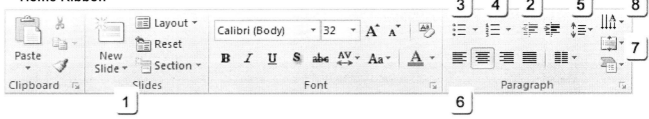

Menu Maps
From the **Home Ribbon**.
1. Home ->Slides-> New Slide, page 56
2. Home ->Paragraph->Increase List Level, page 63
3. Home ->Paragraph->Bullets, page 65
4. Home ->Paragraph->Numbering, page 69
5. Home ->Paragraph->Line Spacing, page 73
6. Home ->Paragraph->Alignment, page 76
7. Home ->Paragraph->Align->Bottom, page 77
8. Home ->Paragraph->Text Direction, page 78

Working with Text

There are several methods for processing information. In general, people focus on either the Text, Pictures, or Music. Microsoft PowerPoint has tools, tools and more tools for formatting the Text. This lesson will look at all of the options available in the **Paragraph** Group. As you go through the various examples ask yourself: what is the purpose of the formatting? Will it draw attention to your message? Is the Text easier to read? Will this formatting improve the show?

Good questions. Let's look for some answers.

Start -> All Programs ->Microsoft Office-> Microsoft Office PowerPoint 2010

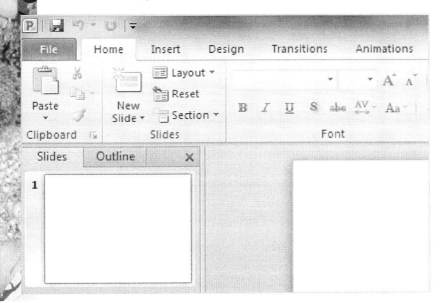

Please Start Microsoft PowerPoint
What do you see at the top of the screen?
Is there a Title Bar that says Microsoft PowerPoint? Yes.

Is there a Home Ribbon with the Clipboard, Font and Paragraph Groups? Yes.

If your screen looks similar to the example on this page, then you are ready to get started.

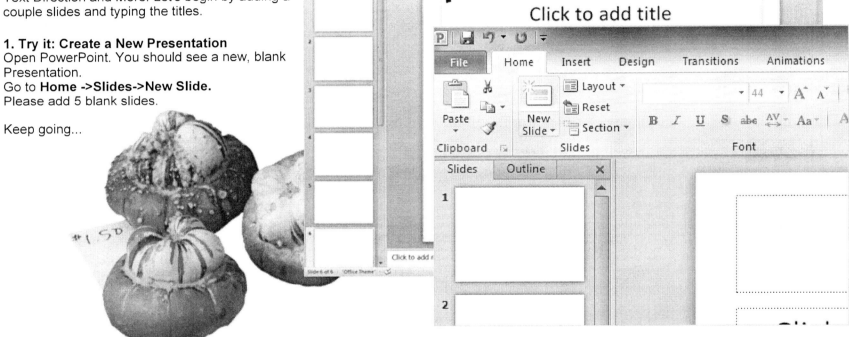

Before You Begin

This lesson will show off the options in the **Paragraph** Group. The options include: Bullets, Indentations, Alignment, Columns, Line Spacing, Text Direction and More. Let's begin by adding a couple slides and typing the titles.

1. Try it: Create a New Presentation

Open PowerPoint. You should see a new, blank Presentation.
Go to **Home ->Slides->New Slide.**
Please add 5 blank slides.

Keep going...

Exam 77-883: Microsoft PowerPoint 2010
2. Creating a Slide Presentation
2.3. Add and remove slides

Enter the Titles

2. Try This: Add Sample Text to the Titles
Select Slide 1, type: Spring Forward, Fall Back
Select Slide 2, type: The Wind Riz, Then it Blew.
Select Slide 3, type: The Rain Friz, Then it
Snew.
Select Slide 4, type: Spring is Gone.
Select Slide 5, type: Fall has Fell,
Select Slide 6, type: Winter is Here...

Keep going...

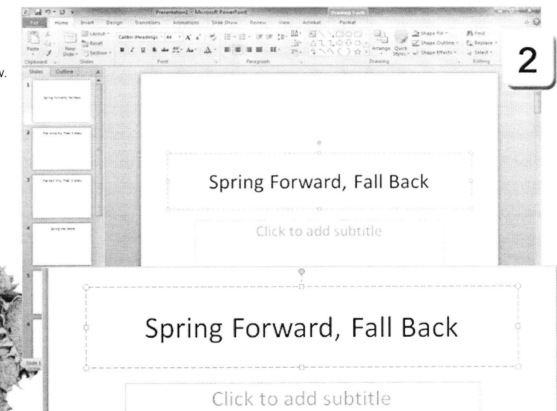

Exam 77-883: Microsoft PowerPoint 2010
2. Creating a Slide Presentation
2.5. Enter and format text

Spelling Checking

Ogden Nash, American poet, liked to play with words such as 'Riz' and 'Friz'. This Spring poem is giving the Microsoft Office **Spell Checker** fits. The Spell Checker has highlighted each word that isn't in the dictionary with a red, wavy line.

What are the options?

3. Try it: Check the Spelling
Go to Slide 2.
Right Click the word: Friz.

What Do You See? The Spell Checker offers several words from the Dictionary. The other options include **Ignore All** and **Add to Dictionary**.

Select **Ignore All**
(The poet spelled 'em rite)
Keep going...!

Review ->Proofing->Spelling

Exam 77-883: Microsoft PowerPoint 2010
6. Collaborating on Presentations
6.2. Apply proofing tools: Use Spelling and Thesaurus features

The Mini Toolbar

When you right-click or highlight the text you may see the **Mini Toolbar**. The Mini Toolbar has a short list of the Font options on the Home Ribbon. The technical term for this is in-place activation.

4. Try it: Format the Title
Go to Slide 6.
Select the word: Winter.

Use the **Mini Toolbar** to format the Font:
Font Style: Italic
Font Color: Blue
Very good.

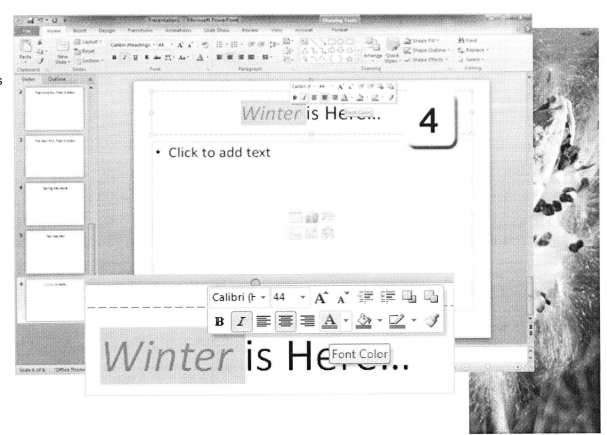

Exam 77-883: Microsoft PowerPoint 2010
2. Creating a Slide Presentation
2.5. Enter and format text: Change Text Format

Use the Outline

With PowerPoint, you can click in the **Text Box** and add text directly to the slides, or you can use the **Outline** to get your thoughts together. You can see the Outline tab in the upper left hand corner.

1. Try it: Use the Outline
Select the **Outline** tab.

What Do You See? The Outline lists all 6 slides in this presentation. You can navigate from one slide to another by clicking on the little slide icon.

Keep going, please...

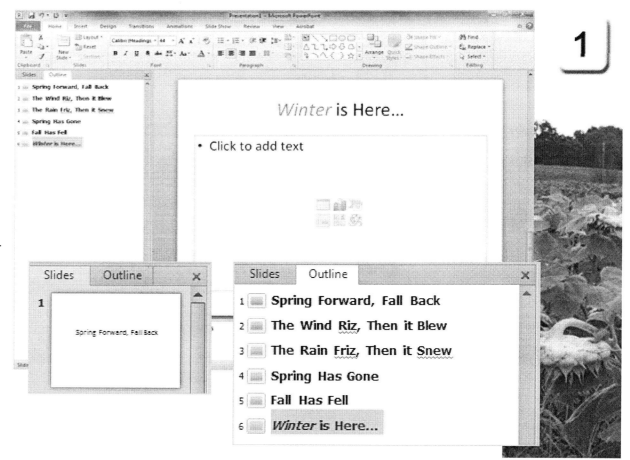

Exam 77-883: Microsoft PowerPoint 2010
2. Creating a Slide Presentation
2.3. Add and remove slides: Use an Outline

Organizing Text

There is something interesting built into the **Outline**. You can organize the slideshow by rearranging the slides. **Drag and drop editing**: it works like moving a picture.

2. Try it: Edit the Outline
Go to Slide 6: Winter is Here..
Click and hold your mouse.
Look for a four-headed **arrow** when you hover over the little slide icon.

As you drag and drop the slide, you should see a horizontal line that lets you know the current position.

Go ahead and scramble the outline.
Then, drag it back to the correct order when you are done practicing. Keep going...

Memo to Self: The arrows in this screen capture have been exaggerated so that you can see them. Your mouse will prolly have a much smaller symbol.

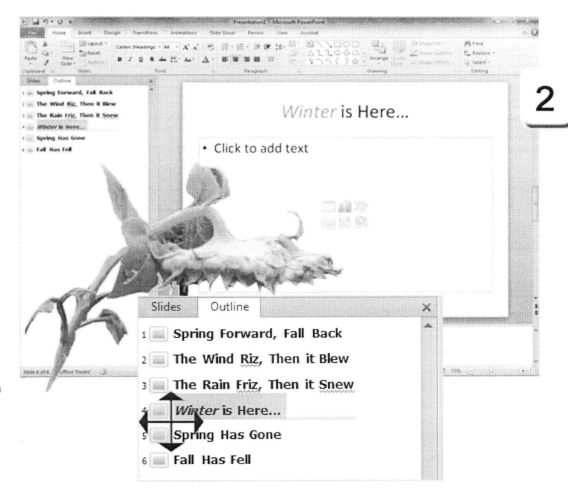

Exam 77-883: Microsoft PowerPoint 2010
2. Creating a Slide Presentation
2.3. Add and remove slides: Use an Outline

Working with the Outline

The text boxes on the slides are dynamic. You can manipulate the text--and which text box it populates--by promoting and demoting the indentation.

3. Before You Begin: Add a new slide
Go to the **Outline** view.
Select Slide 6.
Place your cursor at the end of Slide 6.
Hit the **Enter** key on your keyboard
You should see a new, blank slide.

Type: And it is Colder Than Usual!

What do you see? The text shows up in the outline as well as the Title on the slide.

Keep going, please.

Memo to Self: An Outline is a useful function in both PowerPoint and Word.

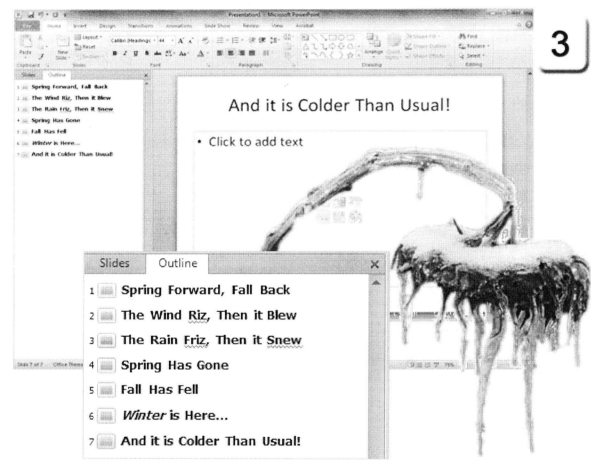

Exam 77-883: Microsoft PowerPoint 2010
2. Creating a Slide Presentation
2.3. Add and remove slides: Use an Outline

Increase and Decrease

Watch what happens when you change the indentation, or **List Level**, on a slide title.

4. Try This: Change the List Level
Go to the **Outline**.
Select Slide 7.
Go to **Home ->Paragraph.**
Click on **Increase List Level.**

What Do You See? When you **Increase the List Level** the title on Slide7 will become the text on Slide 6.

Try it: Decrease or Increase
Use **Decrease List Level** to move the text back to the first level on Slide 7. Keep going...

Home ->Paragraph->Increase List Level

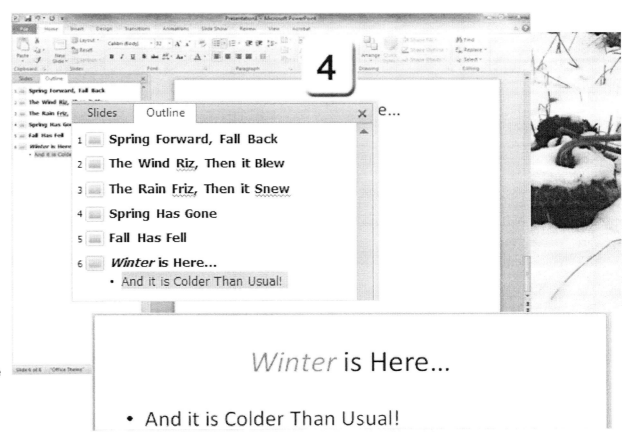

Exam 77-883: Microsoft PowerPoint 2010
2. Creating a Slide Presentation
2.3. Add and remove slides: Use an Outline to Change the List Level

Create Bulleted Lists

Technically, this is called **promoting** or **demoting** the **List Level**. It is done with the **Increase** and **Decrease** options in the **Paragraph** group. You can use these buttons to create bulleted or numbered lists.

1. Try it: Create Bulleted Lists
Click in the bottom Text Box.
Type: January.
Click **Enter** on the keyboard.
Type: February.
Click **Enter** on the keyboard.
Type: March.
Click **Enter** on the keyboard.

What Do You See? Each time you click **Enter** you should see a new bulleted item in the list.

Keep going...

Home ->Paragraph->Increase List Level

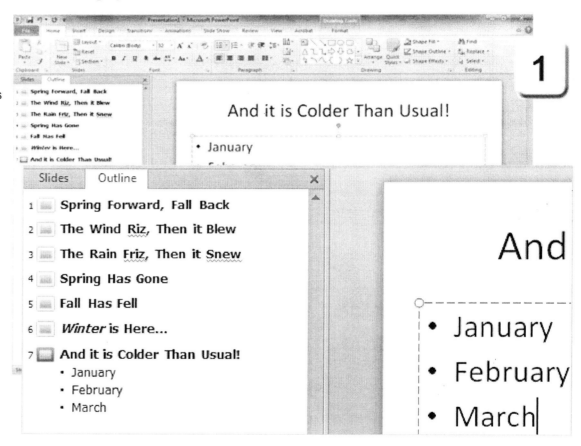

Exam 77-883: Microsoft PowerPoint 2010
2. Creating a Slide Presentation
2.3. Add and remove slides: Use an Outline to Change the List Level

Choose the Bullets

PowerPoint automatically puts bullets in front of the text. It is one of the long-standing jokes that "bullets" is a good name because that's what happens to speakers who use too many of them! <small grin>

You can change the bullets.

2. Try it: Choose the Bullets
Select the type in the Text Box, just as you would highlight text in Word.

Go to **Home ->Paragraph.**
Go to **Bullets and Numbering.**
Select: Filled Square Bullets.

Keep going...

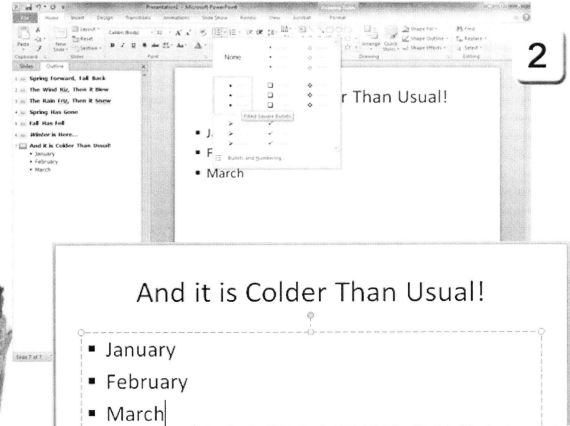

And it is Colder Than Usual!

- January
- February
- March

Exam 77-883: Microsoft PowerPoint 2010
2. Creating a Slide Presentation
2.5. Enter and format text: Change the formatting of Bulleted and Numbered Lists

Format the Bullets

In addition to the circles, squares, check marks and puppy paws, you can choose a different **Symbol** or **Picture** for your bullets.

3. Try This: Format the Bullets
Go to Slide 7. Select the sample text.
Go to **Home -> Paragraph->Bullets.**
Click on **Bullets and Numbering**.

What Do You See? There are two tabs in the pop up window: Bulleted and Numbered.

What Else Do You See? You can edit the **Size** and **Color** of the Bullet or Number.

Keep going...

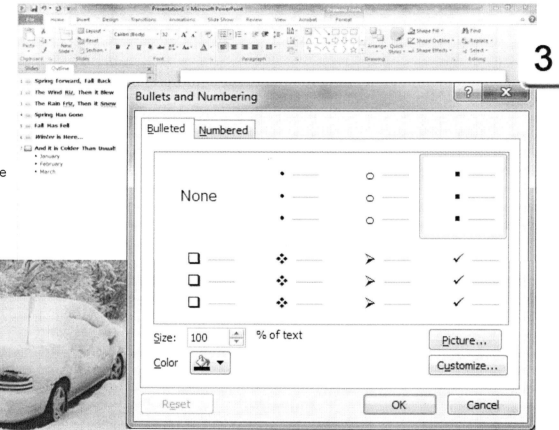

Exam 77-883: Microsoft PowerPoint 2010
2. Creating a Slide Presentation
2.5. Enter and format text: Change the formatting of Bulleted and Numbered Lists

Define the Bullet: Use a Picture

The **Picture** button offers little images that match the Themes in Microsoft Office 2010. You can also select your own picture. Keep it simple!

How Did We Get Here?
Go to Slide 7. Select the sample text.
Go to **Home -> Paragraph->Bullets.**
Go to **Bullets and Numbering.**
Click on **Picture.**

4. What Do You See? When you select **Picture,** you can review the **Picture Bullets** and select one if you wish. Keep going, please.

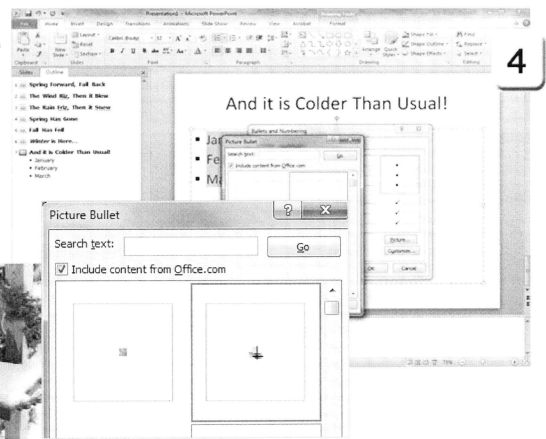

Exam 77-883: Microsoft PowerPoint 2010
2. Creating a Slide Presentation
2.5. Enter and format text: Use a Picture for Bulleted Lists

Define New Bullet:
Use a Symbol or Wingding

5. Try This, Too: Customize the Bullet
Go to Slide 7. Select the sample text.
Go to **Home -> Paragraph->Bullets**.
Go to **Bullets and Numbering**.
Click on **Customize**.

What Do You See? When you click on **Customize**, you can review the **Fonts** and select one. Stars, bars and shapes can be found in Symbols and Wingdings. The screen shot on this page has snowflake symbols.

OK, OK. That's a good review of bullets.

Home ->Paragraph->Bullets->Bullets and Numbering->Customize

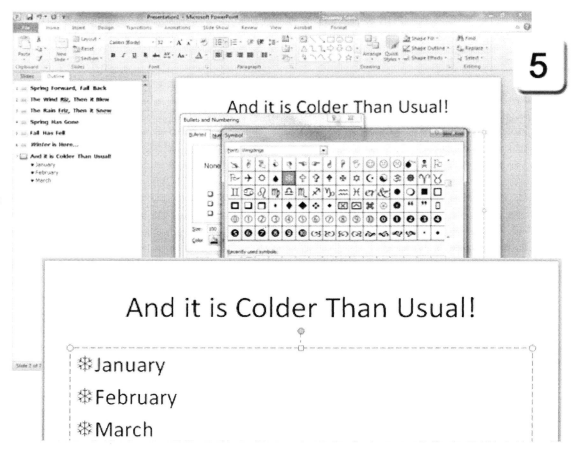

Exam 77-883: Microsoft PowerPoint 2010
2. Creating a Slide Presentation
2.5. Enter and format text: Customize Bulleted and Numbered Lists

Apply Numbers

Many people prefer numbered lists. Here are some **Numbering** options.

1. Try This: Apply a Number Format
Go to Slide 7. Select the sample text.
Go to **Home -> Paragraph**.
Click on **Numbering**.

What Do You See? When you click on **Numbering**, you can review the options in the **Numbering Library**.

Please choose the first number format from the Library. Keep going...

What Else Do You See? If you want to **remove** the Bullets or Numbers, you can select **None** from the Library.

Home ->Paragraph->Numbering

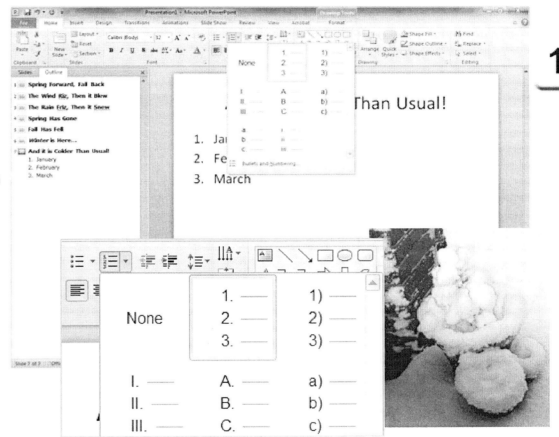

Exam 77-883: Microsoft PowerPoint 2010
2. Creating a Slide Presentation
2.5. Enter and format text: Customize Bulleted and Numbered Lists

Working with Numbers

Different slides in your presentation may need to **Continue** the numbers from a previous list or **Start** the numbers at one, again. Here are the steps.

2. Try This: Change the Numbering
Go to Slide 7. Select the numbered list.
Go to **Home ->Paragraph->Numbering**.
Go to **Bullets and Numbering->Numbered.**
Go to **Start At** and type:9.
Click **OK** and review the results.
The numbered list should start at 9.

Try This, Too: Restart the Numbering at 1
Select the numbered list.
Go to **Home ->Paragraph->Numbering.**
Go to Bullets and Numbering->Numbered.
Go to **Start At** and type:1.
Click **OK** and review the results, please.
The numbered list should start at 1, again.

Keep going...

Home ->Paragraph->Numbering>Bullets and Numbering->Numbered

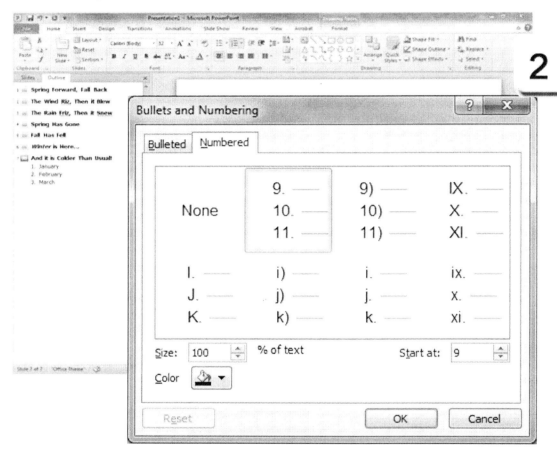

Exam 77-883: Microsoft PowerPoint 2010
2. Creating a Slide Presentation
2.5. Enter and format text: Customize Bulleted and Numbered Lists

Multilevel List Formats

A **Multilevel List** organizes your information into topics and subtopics. These lists can be formatted with the **Increase** and **Decrease** buttons in the **Paragraph** Group that we looked at before.

3. Try It: Create a Multilevel List
Go to Slide 7.
Place your cursor after March.
Type: Comes In Like a Lion
Go to **Home ->Paragraph->Increase List**.

What Do You See? The new type is now indented under March on Slide 7.

Try This, Too: Add to the List
Place your cursor after: Comes in Like a Lion.
Click **Enter** to add a new item.
Type: And Goes Out Like a Lamb.

Keep going...

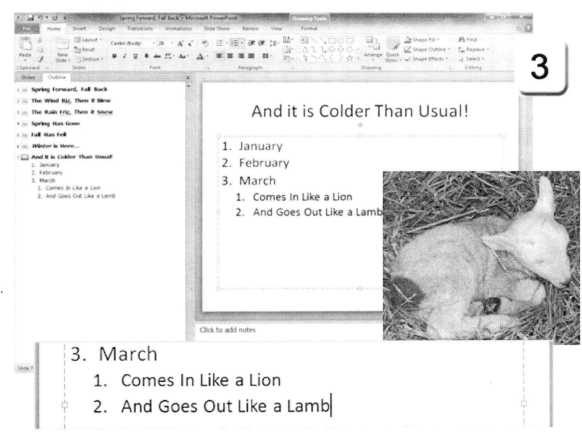

Exam 77-883: Microsoft PowerPoint 2010
2. Creating a Slide Presentation
2.5. Enter and format text: Customize Bulleted and Numbered Lists

More Number Options

Say you wanted the indented items to be formatted differently than the numbered style. Let's look at the options.

4. Try it: Format the Multilevel List

Select the last two items, only.
Go to **Home ->Paragraph->Numbering**.
Go to
Select: a), b), c)

What Do You See? The indented text is formatted with letters. If you add another item it will be numbered with c).

OK, that's enough about numbers.

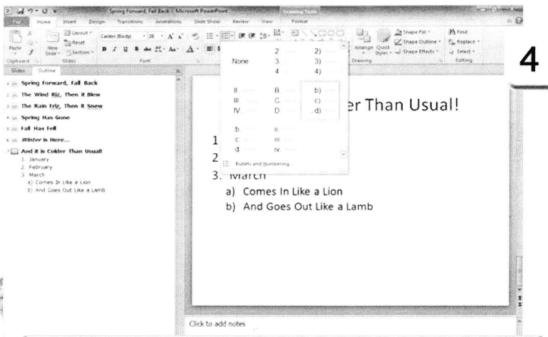

3. March
   a) Comes In Like a Lion
   b) And Goes Out Like a Lamb

Exam 77-883: Microsoft PowerPoint 2010
2. Creating a Slide Presentation
2.5. Enter and format text: Customize Bulleted and Numbered Lists

Format the Line Spacing

The amount of space between two lines of type is called **leading**. Think back to the days when type was set in wooden presses. Thin blocks of lead were placed between the letters so that the "Descenders" (the parts of the letter that go below the line) do not touch the "Ascenders" (the top parts of the letter.)

Microsoft PowerPoint uses **Line Spacing** to edit the leading between the paragraphs.

5. Try it: Format the Line Spacing
Go to Slide 7. Select the list.
Go to **Home ->Paragraph->Line Spacing**.

What Do You See? The Live Preview lets you see the difference between 1.0 and 3.0.

Keep going...

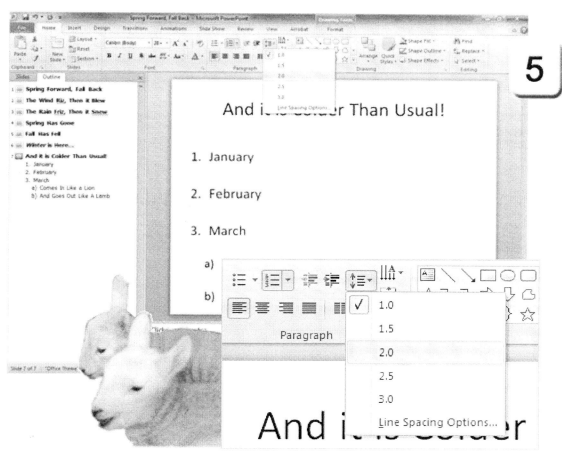

Exam 77-883: Microsoft PowerPoint 2010
2. Creating a Slide Presentation
2.5. Enter and format text: Paragraph Line Spacing

More Line Spacing Options

The 1.0, 2.0 and 3.0 leading are the default **Line Spacing**. You can edit the **Indents** and **Spacing** if you wish.

6. Try it: Format the Line Spacing Options
Go to Slide 7 and select the numbered list.
Go to **Home ->Paragraph->Line Spacing.**
Click on **Line Spacing Options.**

Try This, Too: Edit the Indents and Spacing
Alignment: Left

In Indentation, edit the following:
Before Text: (This is blank because our list has different formatting for the two List Levels.
Special: Hanging **By**: 0.56

In Spacing, edit the following:
Before: 3 pt
After: 0 pt
Line Spacing: Multiple **At**: 1.8
Click **OK** and keep going...

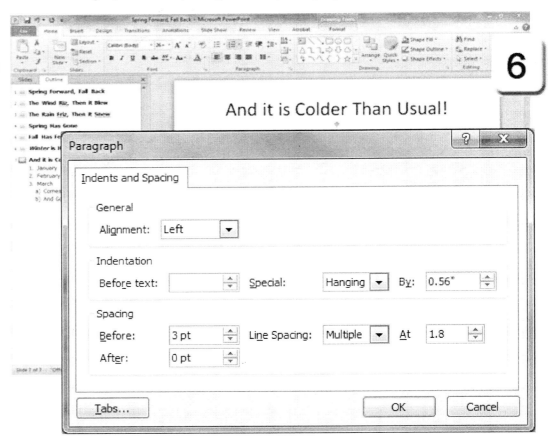

Exam 77-883: Microsoft PowerPoint 2010
2. Creating a Slide Presentation
2.5. Enter and format text: Paragraph Line Spacing

Positioning the Text

There are two different alignment options that edit the position of the text. First, the Paragraph **Alignment** formats the text: left, right, center and justified.

Before You Begin: Add Sample Text
Go to Slide 6. Add the following:
Let it snow!
Let it snow!
Let it snow!

Select each phrase and edit the List Level:
Go to **Home ->Paragraph.**
Click on **Increase List Level.**

What Do You See? Each time you increase the **List Level** the text is indented more. The text is also a smaller point size. The bullet is different as well.

Keep going...

Home ->Paragraph->Increase List Level

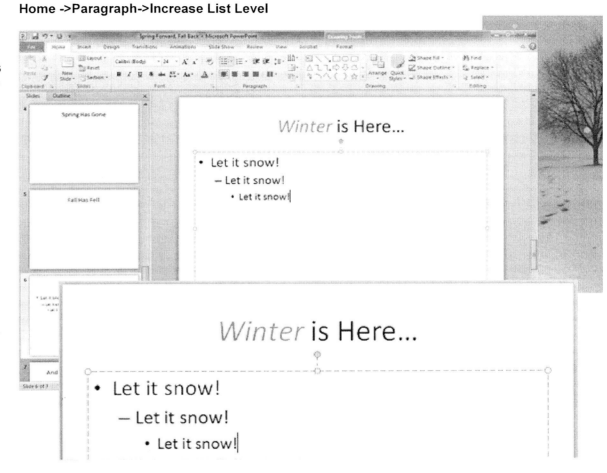

Exam 77-883: Microsoft PowerPoint 2010
2. Creating a Slide Presentation
2.5. Enter and format text: Change the formatting of Bulleted and Numbered Lists

Paragraph Alignment

7. Try it: Format the Alignment
Select the first paragraph: Let it Snow!
Go to **Home ->Paragraph->Alignment**.
Select **Center**.

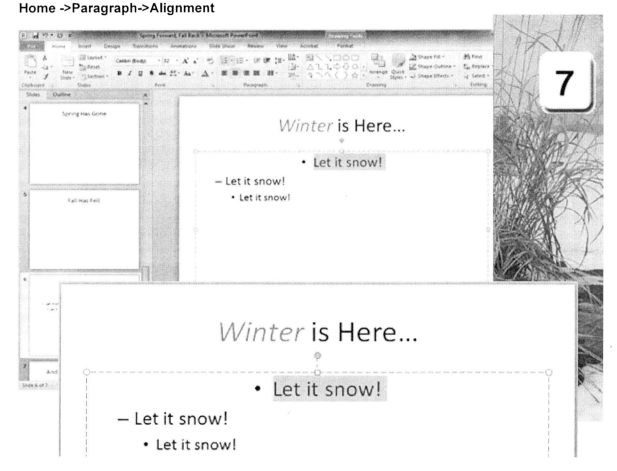

What Do You See? The text, as well as the bullet formatting, should be centered in the Text Box.

What Else Do You See? This formatting is applied only to the text that you select.

Try This, Too: Format the Other Text
Select the other two paragraphs.
Go to **Home ->Paragraph->Alignment**.
Select **Center**.

Please keep going...there's more.

Exam 77-883: Microsoft PowerPoint 2010
2. Creating a Slide Presentation
2.5. Enter and format text.: Alignment: Left, Right, Center

Text Alignment

The second **Alignment** option positions all of the text within the Text Box: Top, Middle Bottom. Here are the steps.

8. Try it: Align the Text
Go to Slide 6.
Select the text: Let it snow!
Go to **Home ->Paragraph->Align**.
Click on **Bottom**.

What Do You See? All of the paragraphs should be placed in the bottom of the Text Box.

The paragraphs cannot be formatted independently: one on top and another in the middle. This formatting applies to all of the text within the Text Box.

Keep going...there's one more to go!

Home ->Paragraph->Align->Bottom

Exam 77-883: Microsoft PowerPoint 2010
2. Creating a Slide Presentation
2.6. Format text boxes: Set the Alignment Top, Middle, Bottom

Text Direction

This last option is fun: **Text Direction**.

9. Try it: Edit the Text Direction
Go to Slide 3.
Add the text: Rain, Rain, Go Away
Go to **Home ->Paragraph.**
Click on **Text Direction**.

What Do You See? The options are:
Horizontal
Rotate all text 90
Rotate all text 270
Stacked
More Options.

The Computer Mama Sez: Go ahead.
Play with the button and watch the text
rotate. Way cool.

Exam 77-883: Microsoft PowerPoint 2010
2. Creating a Slide Presentation
2.5. Enter and format text.: Text Direction

Save Your Work

This little presentation will be used in the next lesson that looks at the **Drawing** tools that are available for formatting the **Text Box**.

Try it: Save Your Work
1. Go to **File->Save**.
2. Browse to your Documents folder.
3. Fill in the blanks
File Name: Spring Forward, Fall Back.
Save As Type: PowerPoint Presentation.

Click **SAVE**.

File ->Save

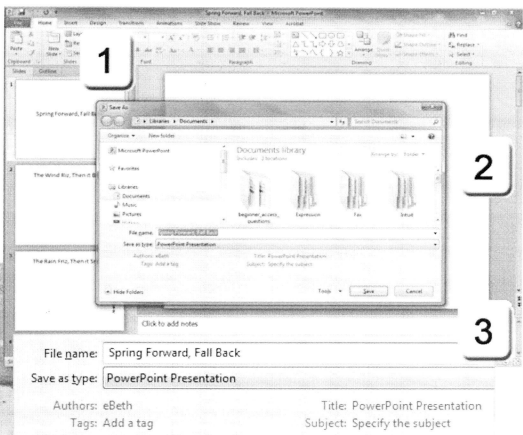

File name:	Spring Forward, Fall Back		
Save as type:	PowerPoint Presentation		
Authors: eBeth		Title: PowerPoint Presentation	
Tags: Add a tag		Subject: Specify the subject	

Exam 77-883: Microsoft PowerPoint 2010
1. Managing the PowerPoint Environment
1.4. Configure PowerPoint file options: Save a presentation

P is for Paragraph

This lesson walked through the options in the **Paragraph** Group:
Bullets and Numbering
Lists and editing the List Level
Line Spacing
Alignment (Left, Right, Center)
Align (Top, Middle, Bottom)

OK, that's enough for now.

You done good.
You get the cookie.

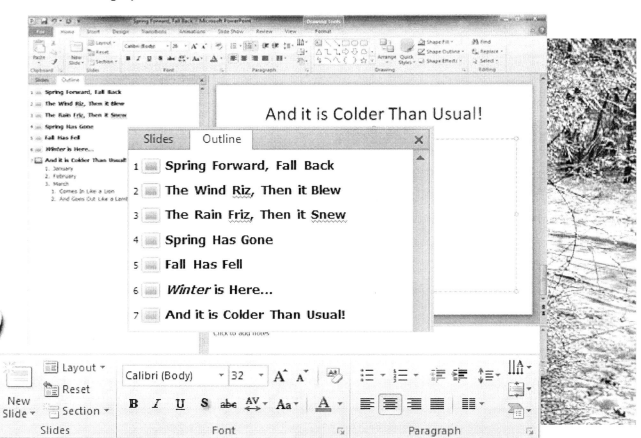

Practice Activities

Lesson 3: P is for Paragraph

Try This: Do the following steps

1. Open a new blank presentation
2. On the Title Slide put the Title: Your New Computer
3. Add a new slide and add the title text: Windows.
4. In the content text box on Slide 2, add the following list of items.
   a. XP
   b. Vista
   c. 7
   d. 8
5. Format the bullets on Slide 2 to be a shape of your choice
6. Add a new slide. Add the title: Software.
   a. Align the title on Slide 3 to be set as Alignment Right
   b. Add the following items to the content box on Slide 3:
      i. Microsoft Office
      ii. Word
      iii. Excel
      iv. PowerPoint
   c. One slide 3, demote Word, Excel and PowerPoint to be 1 list level lower
   d. One slide 3, Format the line spacing to 1.5

7. Add a new slide. Add the title: Hardware
   a. On slide 4, add the following list:
      i. Monitor
      ii. Keyboard
      iii. Mouse
   b. On slide 4, Remove the bullet points
   c. On slide 4, Chance the Text Direction to stacked
   d. On slide 4, make the font size of the list smaller by 2 sizes using the Decrease font size command
8. Using the outline view, move the Hardware slide to be slide 2
9. Save this file as Beginning PowerPoint Practice Activity 2

Test Yourself

1. The Paragraph group is located on which Ribbon?
a. Font
b. Insert
c. Format
d. Home
Tip: Beginning PowerPoint, page 56

2. When does the Mini Toolbar appear?
a. When text is selected or highlighted
b. Go to File--> Options--> View Mini Toolbar
c. Go to View--> Mini Toolbar
Tip: Beginning PowerPoint, page 59

3. Which are Slide Views?
(Give all correct answers.)
a. Outline
b. Slide
c. Transition
Tip: Beginning PowerPoint, page 60

4. Which of the following are true?
(Give all correct answers)
a. You can drag and drop slides in Outline View
b. Text added to the outline appears on a slide
c. Decrease List Level on a slide title makes the text appear on the previous title
Tip: Beginning PowerPoint, page 61-62

5. Increase and Decrease List Level work on which of the following?
(Give all correct answers.)
a. Slide titles
b. Numbered Lists
c. Bulleted lists
Tip: Beginning PowerPoint, page 63-64

6. Which of the following are bullet options?
(Give all correct answers)
a. Change shape
b. Use a picture
c. Change color
d. Change size
Tip: Beginning PowerPoint, page 66

8. Which of the following are alignment options?
(Give all correct answers)
a. Center
b. Right
c. Left
d. Justified
e. Top
f. Bottom
g. Middle
Tip: Beginning PowerPoint, page 76-77

9. Which are text direction options?
(Give all correct answers)
a. Horizontal
b. Stacked
c. Rotate all text 90 degrees
d. Rotate all text 270 degrees
e. Upside down
Tip: Beginning PowerPoint, page 78

10. Which commands are in the Paragraph group? (Give all correct answers)
a. Align Bottom
b. Center Align
c. Line Spacing
Tip: Beginning PowerPoint, page 73, 76, 77

Take Two

PowerPoint 2010: Creating a Presentation

Text Boxes and Themes

Beginning PowerPoint Objectives
In this lesson, you will learn how to:

1. Identify and use the **Drawing** tools to apply formatting to a **Text Box**

2. Format the Text Box with **Quick Styles**

3. Create a custom Text Box by editing the Shape Fill with Color, Gradient, Texture, Patterns and Pictures

4. Format the Color, Weight and Style of the Text Box **Outline**

5. Work with **Shape Effects**: Shadow, Glow, and 3D Rotation

© 2011 Comma Productions LLC

Lesson 4 : Text Boxes and Themes

1. Readings
Read Lesson 4 in the PowerPoint guide, page 83-120.

Project
A simple presentation that uses the **Drawing** tools to format 4 slides.

Downloads
SummerFlower1.gif
SummerFlower2.gif
SummerFlower3.gif
Song of Solomon.pptx (Completed)
Do You Have One.pptx

2. Practice
Do the Practice Activity on page 121.

3. Assessment
Review the Test questions on page 122.

Home Ribbon

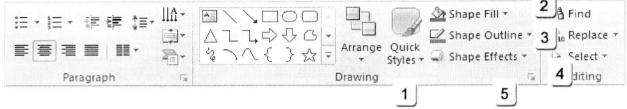

Design Ribbon

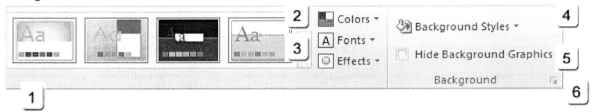

Menu Maps
From the **Home Ribbon**.
1. Home ->Drawing->Quick Styles, page 91
2. Home ->Drawing->Shape Fill, page 94
3. Home ->Drawing->Shape Outline, page 102
4. Home ->Drawing->Shape Effects, page 104
5. Home ->Drawing->Format Shape, page 107

More Menu Maps
From the **Design Ribbon**.
1. Design ->Themes, page 110
2. Design ->Theme->Colors, page 113
3. Design ->Theme->Font, page 115
4. Design->Background->Background Styles, page 117
5. Design ->Background->Hide Background Graphics, page 118
6. Design->Background->More, page 119

Working with Text Boxes

By definition, a **Text Box** is a **Shape**. A Text Box has specific formatting because it is working with Text. Nevertheless, a Text Box is still a Shape, with or without a bulleted list or a Title. Shapes have Outlines, Fill, and Styles. Shapes are formatted with the **Drawing Tools**. This lesson begins with the short stack of **Drawing Tools** on the **Home Ribbon**. Then, we'll review the **Drawing Ribbon** and find a few more options.

Start -> All Programs ->Microsoft Office-> Microsoft Office PowerPoint 2010

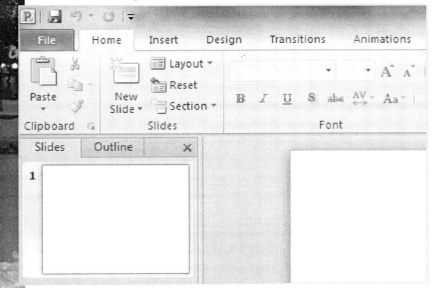

Please Start Microsoft PowerPoint
What do you see at the top of the screen? Is there a Title Bar that says Microsoft PowerPoint? Yes.

Is there a **Home** Ribbon with the Clipboard, Font and Paragraph Groups? Yes.

If your screen looks similar to the example on this page, then you are ready to get started.

Before You Begin

This lesson will demonstrate the **Drawing** tools. The options include Quick Styles, Shape Fill, Shape Outline, and Shape Effects. We will also look at the PowerPoint **Themes**.

1. Try it: Create a New Presentation
Open PowerPoint. You should see a new, blank presentation.
Go to **Home ->Slides->New Slide**
Please add three new slides.

Keep going...

Memo to Self: You do not have to MATCH the images and special effects shown on these pages.

Please add your own pictures if you wish. It is more important that you begin with something and try the options that are available.

Home ->Slides->New Slide

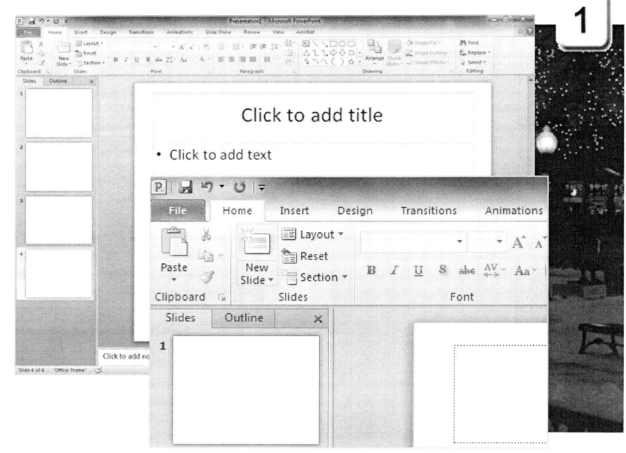

Exam 77-883: Microsoft PowerPoint 2010
2. Creating a Slide Presentation
2.5. Enter and format text

Enter the Titles

2. Try This: Add Text to the Titles

Slide 1, type: Song of Solomon
Slide 2, type: For, Lo, the Winter is Past
Slide 3, type: The Rain is Over and Gone
Slide 4, type: The Flowers Appear on the Earth

Keep going...

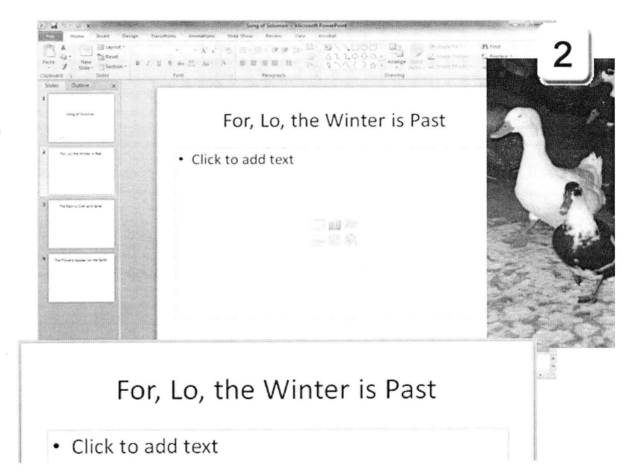

Exam 77-883: Microsoft PowerPoint 2010
2. Creating a Slide Presentation
2.5. Enter and format text

Format the Text

3. Try it: Format the Paragraph
Go to Slide 2.
Select the bottom Text Box.
Type: Winter.

What Do You See? By default, the Text will have a bullet.

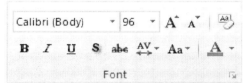

Try This, Too: Format the Font
Select the text: Winter
Go to **Home->Font->Paragraph**.
Click on **Bullet**.
Go to **Home Font->Size**.
Select: 96.

What Do You See? The Text should be large, aligned left, no bullet.
Keep going...

Home ->Font

Exam 77-883: Microsoft PowerPoint 2010
2. Creating a Slide Presentation
2.5. Enter and format text: Change the formatting of Bulleted or Numbered Text

Hello, Drawing Tools

When you click on a **Text Box** to type some words, you will see the outline of the **Shape**. The outline is a dashed blue line with handles on the sides and in each corner. Shapes are formatted with the **Drawing Tools**.

4. Try it: Find the Drawing Tools
Select the bottom Text Box: Winter.

What Do You See? The Home Ribbon has a set of Drawing Tools that include:
Shapes
Arrange
Quick Styles
Shape Fill
Shape Outline
Shape Effects

Keep going...this is getting interesting.

Exam 77-883: Microsoft PowerPoint 2010
2. Creating a Slide Presentation
2.6. Format text boxes: Drawing Tools

And Hello, Drawing Tools
5. Try it: Find More Drawing Tools
The **Drawing Tools Ribbon** has more options in the Groups than the short set on the **Home Ribbon**.

The **Format** Groups include:
Insert Shapes
Shape Styles
WordArt Styles
Arrange
Size

This example will play with the options on the Home Ribbon, first.

Keep going...

Drawing Tools->Format

Exam 77-883: Microsoft PowerPoint 2010
2. Creating a Slide Presentation
2.6. Format text boxes: The Drawing Ribbon

Drawing: Quick Styles

Quick Styles format many aspects of the Text Box including the Shape Fill, Outline, and Effects.

1. Try it: Apply Quick Styles
Go to Slide 2.
Select the bottom Text Box.
Go to **Home ->Drawing.**
Click on **Quick Styles.**
Select: Intense Effect-Blue, Accent 1

What Do You See? As you run over the **Quick Styles** the Font changes from black To white, depending on the Fill Color.

Keep going...

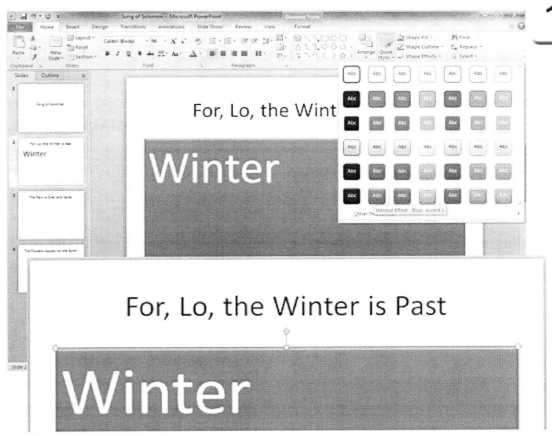

Exam 77-883: Microsoft PowerPoint 2010
2. Creating a Slide Presentation
2.6. Format text boxes: Drawing Quick Styles

Quick Style Options

Every Microsoft Office menu has more goodies at the bottom of the list. The **Quick Styles** has **Other Theme Fills**.

2. Try it: Find Other Theme Fills
Go to Slide 2.
Select the bottom Text Box.
Go to **Home ->Drawing->Quick Styles**.
Click on **Other Theme Fills**.
Select: Style 11

What Do You See? There are various **Gradient Fills**. Look carefully. The second row has a shine at the top. The third row radiates out from the middle.

OK, that's Quick Styles.

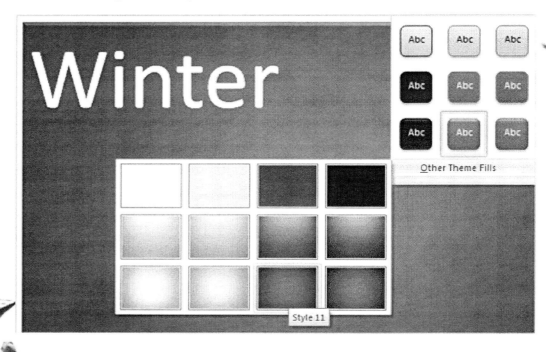

Exam 77-883: Microsoft PowerPoint 2010
2. Creating a Slide Presentation
2.6. Format text boxes: Drawing Quick Styles

Drawing: Shape Fill

As you saw on the previous pages, Quick Styles format a bunch of Text Box features. Let's look at the options one at a time and see how they work.

1. Before You Begin: Enter the Text
Go to Slide 3.
Select the bottom Text Box.
Type: Spring.

Try This, Too: Format the Font
Select the text: Spring
Go to **Home->Font->Paragraph.**
Click on Bullet.
Go to **Home Font->Size.**
Select: 96.

Keep going...

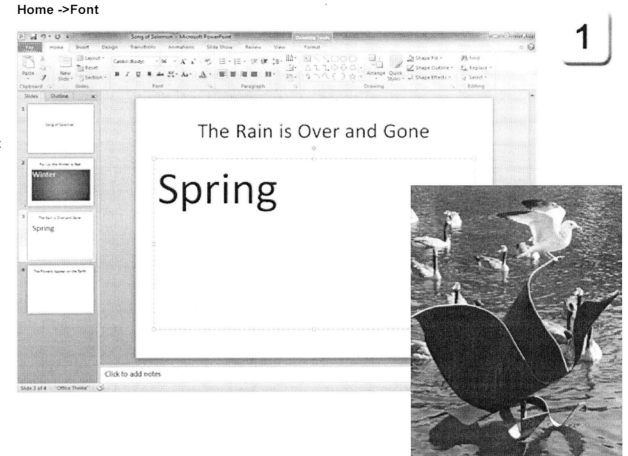

Exam 77-883: Microsoft PowerPoint 2010
2. Creating a Slide Presentation
2.5. Enter and format text: Change the formatting of Bulleted or Numbered Text

Shape Fill: Color

The **Shape Fill** can be a color, picture, gradient or Texture. Let's start with color.

2. Try it: Edit the Color of the Shape Fill
Go to Slide 3.
Select the bottom Text Box.
Go to **Home ->Drawing->Shape Fill.**
Select: Olive Green, Accent 3, Lighter 40%.

What Do You See? The Shape Fill has a pallet of **Theme Colors**.

The **Standard Colors** (red, yellow, green, blue, etc) are also available.

Keep going...

Exam 77-883: Microsoft PowerPoint 2010
2. Creating a Slide Presentation
2.6. Format text boxes: Shape Fill-Color

Shape Fill: Texture

The **Texture** gallery includes cloth, granite, paper and wood. Each texture applies a different meaning to the Text Box. For example, a bank would use marble to say that they are solid. A day care center may use cloth or denim to suggest comfort.

3. Try it: Edit the Fill Texture
Go to Slide 3.
Select the bottom Text Box.
Go to **Home ->Drawing->Shape Fill.**
Go to **Texture.**

Keep going...

Home ->Drawing->Shape Fill->Texture

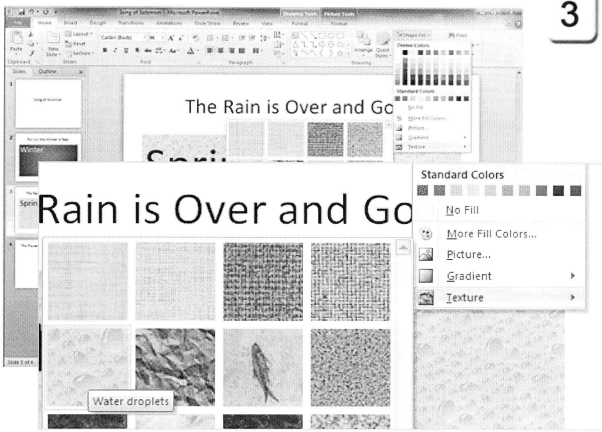

Exam 77-883: Microsoft PowerPoint 2010
2. Creating a Slide Presentation
2.6. Format text boxes: Shape Fill-Texture

Shape Fill: Gradient

A **Gradient** is a method for creating a gradual change in the intensity of the color. The Gradient has a start (top, center, bottom) and a direction.

4. Try it: Edit the Fill Gradient
Go to Slide 3.
Select the bottom Text Box.
Go to **Home ->Drawing->Shape Fill**.
Go to **Gradient**.

Where Have You Seen This Before?
The **Gradient** gallery has more choices than the Quick Styles. The options include Light and Dark Variations.

Keep going...

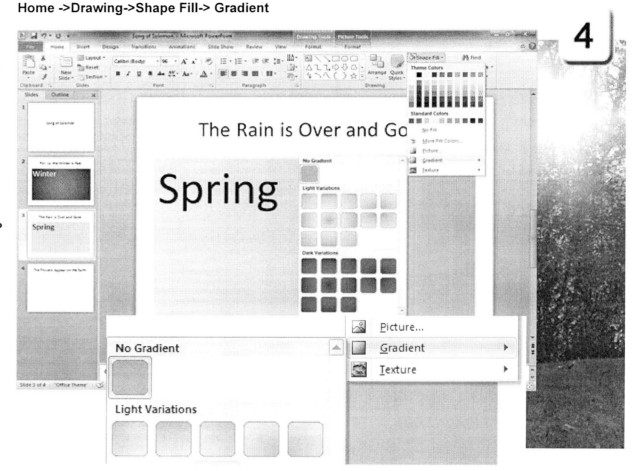

Exam 77-883: Microsoft PowerPoint 2010
2. Creating a Slide Presentation
2.6. Format text boxes: Shape Fill-Gradient

More Gradient Options

5. Try it: Review the Format Options
Go to Slide 3.
Select the bottom Text Box.
Go to **Home ->Drawing->Shape Fill**.
Go to **Gradient->More Gradients.**

What Do You See? When you click on
More Gradients, you will see the options
for Formatting a Shape. They are:
No Fill
Solid Fill
Gradient
Picture of Texture
Pattern Fill
Slide Background.

Then what? Keep going...

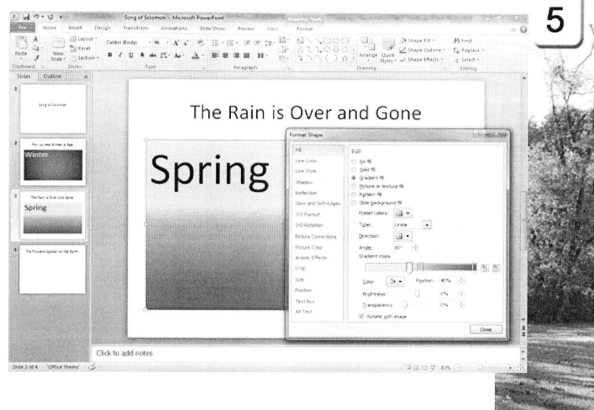

Exam 77-883: Microsoft PowerPoint 2010
2. Creating a Slide Presentation
2.6. Format text boxes: Shape Fill-Gradient

Shape Fill: Gradient Stops

You can edit every aspect of the Gradient if you wish. Here is one option that has interesting results.

6. Try it: Edit the Gradient Fill
Please select the following.
Fill: Gradient fill.
Preset colors: Moss

By default the **Type** is Linear and the **Angle** is 90 degrees.

Try This, Too: Edit the Gradient Stops
There are two Gradient stops in this example. If you slide the left stop towards the center, there will be more light color at the top of the slide.

Go ahead, play with the Color, Brightness and Transparency. If you don't like the formatting, you can always UNDO.

OK, keep going...!

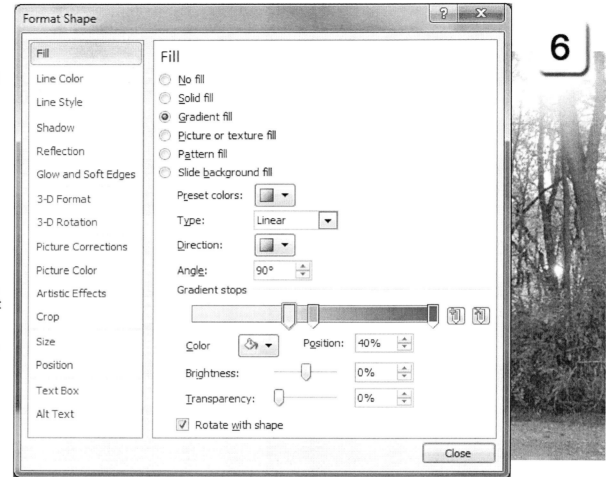

Exam 77-883: Microsoft PowerPoint 2010
2. Creating a Slide Presentation
2.6. Format text boxes: Shape Fill-Gradient

Shape Fill: Picture
While we're here, let's try using a **Picture** for the Shape Fill.

7. Try This: Edit the Text
Go to Slide 4.
Select the bottom Text Box.
Type: Flowers Appear.

Try This, Too: Format the Font
Select the text: Flowers Appear
Go to **Home->Font->Paragraph**.
Click on **Bullet**.
Go to **Home Font->Size**.
Select: 96.

Keep going...what is next, we wonder?

Exam 77-883: Microsoft PowerPoint 2010
2. Creating a Slide Presentation
2.6. Format text boxes: Shape Fill-Picture

Home ->Drawing->Shape Fill->Picture

Shape Fill: Find a Picture

8. Try This: Use a Picture for the Fill
Go to **Home ->Drawing->Shape Fill**.
Click on **Picture.**
You will be prompted to **Browse** for a picture. The example on the page is called SummerFlower2.jpg

Keep going...!

Memo to Self: You do not have to MATCH the images and special effects shown on these pages. Please add your own pictures if you wish.

Exam 77-883: Microsoft PowerPoint 2010
2. Creating a Slide Presentation
2.6. Format text boxes: Shape Fill-Picture

Working with the Picture Fill

The **Text Box** now has a **Picture Fill** behind the text. By default, the text is black, however it seems a little hard to read. A little bit of formatting can make the text stand out.

9. Try it: Format the Font Shadow
Select the words: Flowers Appear.
Go to **Home ->Font->Shadow**.

Memo to Self: You may want to change the Font Color or Size, depending on the picture you chose for the Shape Fill. Do whatever it takes to make the message easier to read.

Exam 77-883: Microsoft PowerPoint 2010
2. Creating a Slide Presentation
2.6. Format text boxes: Shape Fill-Picture

Shape Outline: Color

Each Shape has an **Outline** that you can edit if you wish. You can format the Color, Weight and Style.

1. Try it: Format the Shape Outline
Begin on Slide 4.
Select the Text Box.
Go to **Home ->Drawing**.
Go to **Shape Outline**.
Select a **Theme Color**.

Keep going...

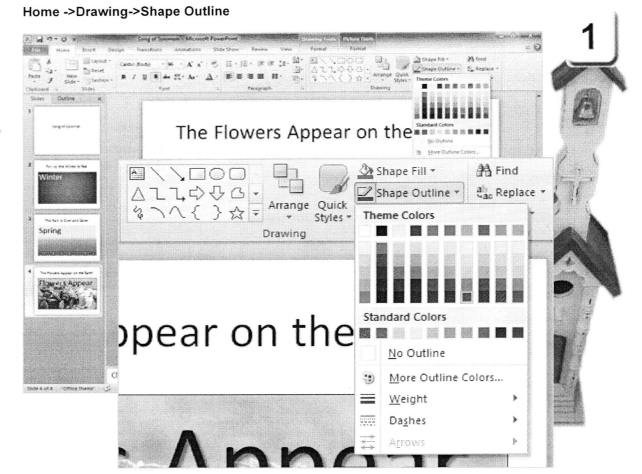

Exam 77-883: Microsoft PowerPoint 2010
2. Creating a Slide Presentation
2.6. Format text boxes: Shape Outline Color, Weight, Style

Shape Outline: Options

You can use the **Drawing** tools to edit the Outline Weight and Style as well.

2. Try it: Edit the Weight and Style
Continuing with Slide 4.
The Text Box is selected.
Go to **Home ->Drawing**.
Go to **Shape Outline**.
Select a **Weight**: 3 pt.

Go to **Home ->Drawing**.
Go to **Shape Outline->Dashes**.
Select: Round dot.

Maybe...Maybe not.
You can UNDO the Round dots.

Turn the page for more...

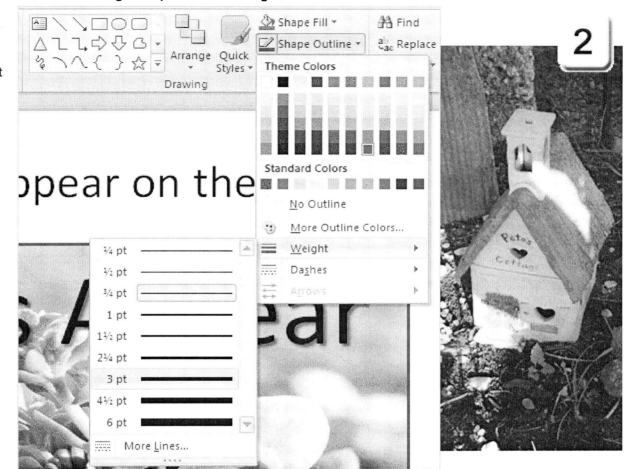

Exam 77-883: Microsoft PowerPoint 2010
2. Creating a Slide Presentation
2.6. Format text boxes: Shape Outline Color, Weight, Style

Shape Effects: Shadow

Microsoft PowerPoint has wonderful **Shape Effects**. The options include Shadow, Reflection, Glow, Soft Edges, Bevel and 3-D Rotation.

A **Shadow** brings an image out from the background. We added a shadow on the Text. Here are the steps to add a shadow to the Text Box.

3. Try it: Add a Shadow
Continuing with Slide 4.
The Text Box is selected.
Go to **Home ->Drawing**.
Go to **Shape Effects->Shadow**.

What Do You See? There are several types of **Shadows.** The **Outer Shadows** are applied outside of the Shape. The **Inner Shadows** create the illusion of depth, like shiny candy.

Please pick one of the **Shadows.**
Keep going...

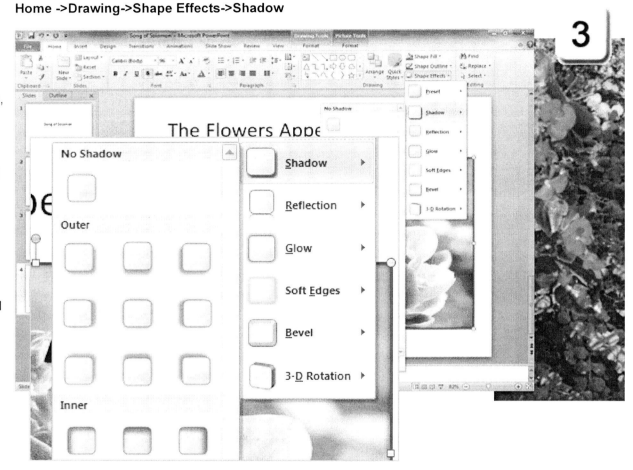

Exam 77-883: Microsoft PowerPoint 2010
2. Creating a Slide Presentation
2.6. Format text boxes: Shape Effects-Shadow

Shape Effects: Glow

A **Glow** is a Shape Effect which is applied outside of the Text Box. There are several **Glow Variations** from Subtle to Intense.

4. Try it: Add a Glow
Continuing with Slide 4.
The Text Box is selected.
Go to **Home ->Drawing**.
Go to **Shape Effects->Glow**.

What Do You See? You can edit the Glow Colors if you wish.

Please select a **Glow Variation**.
Keep going...!

Exam 77-883: Microsoft PowerPoint 2010
2. Creating a Slide Presentation
2.6. Format text boxes: Shape Effects-Glow

Shape Effects: 3D

Now, let's talk about some seriously creative options in the **3D-Effects**. Here we go.

5. Try it: Add a 3d-Effect
Still on Slide 4.
The Text Box is selected.
Go to **Home ->Drawing**.
Go to **Shape Effects->3D-Rotation**.

What Do You See? The 3D options are:
Parallel: The sides go the same direction.

Perspective: The sides of the Shape aim at a vanishing point.

Oblique: The effect is applied to one side.

Select a **Rotation** if you wish.

What Else Do You See? You may need to resize the Text Box after you add a 3D Effect so that it fits on the slide.

Home ->Drawing->Shape Effects->3D-Rotation

Exam 77-883: Microsoft PowerPoint 2010
2. Creating a Slide Presentation
2.6. Format text boxes: Shape Effects-3D Effects

More Shape Formats

There are more options for formatting a Shape than are shown on in **Drawing** Group on the **Home** Ribbon. Look at the bottom right corner of the Drawing Group for a small arrow. That arrow always gives you **More**. Let's look at what's available.

1. Try it: Find the Option Arrow
Begin on Slide 1.
Select the Title Text Box.
Go to **Home ->Drawing.**
Click on **Format Shape.**
(That's the small arrow in the corner.)

Keep going...

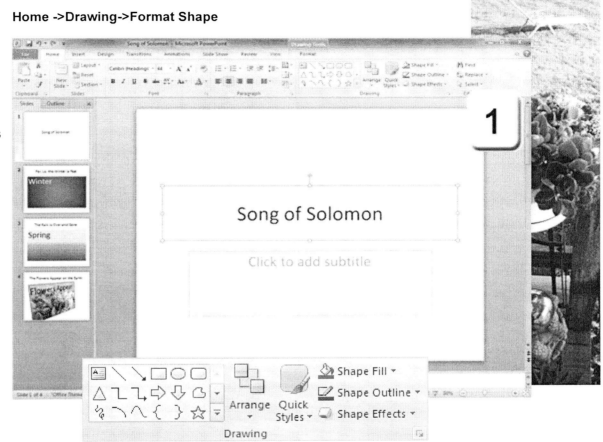

Exam 77-883: Microsoft PowerPoint 2010
2. Creating a Slide Presentation
2.6. Format text boxes: Format Shape

Format Shape Dialogue

2. Try it: Review the Options

The formatting choices are listed in categories on the left side of the Dialogue box. The list includes many of the formats we applied with the Drawing Group on the Home Ribbon.

By default, a Text Box is a simple Shape. There is No fill.

You can format the Text Box by selecting a category and making your choices. The Live Preview lets you see your choices immediately.

Let's try something that isn't available on the Home Ribbon.

Keep going, please...

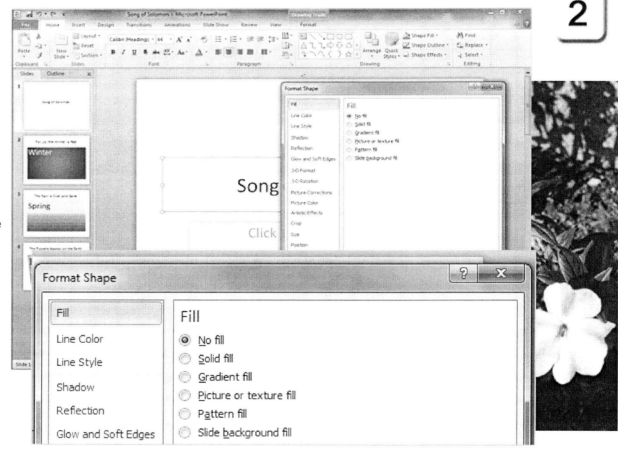

Exam 77-883: Microsoft PowerPoint 2010
2. Creating a Slide Presentation
2.6. Format text boxes: Format Shape Dialogue

Format Shape: Pattern

3. Try it: Create a Custom Fill
We are still on Slide 1.
The Title Text Box is selected.
The **Format Shape** dialogue is open.

Select a Category: **Fill**.
Select a Fill: **Pattern Fill**.

What Do You See? When you select a Pattern Fill you will see the editing options on the bottom.

Try This, Too: Edit the Pattern Fill
Select a Foreground Color: Light Green
Select a Background Color: White
Click **Close** when you are done editing.

OK, that was interesting.

Memo to Self: The Pattern Fills go way, way back to the early days in computers before the screens and printouts had color. Think about it: the first PCs and MACS were black and white in 1984.

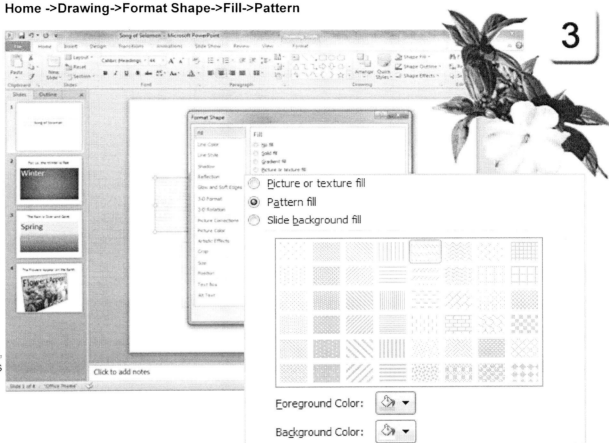

Exam 77-883: Microsoft PowerPoint 2010
2. Creating a Slide Presentation
2.6. Format text boxes: Use Pattern or Texture Fill

Presentation Designs

The previous pages focused on the options for formatting Text Boxes. Slides can be formatted as well. Look on the **Design** Ribbon and you will see the **Themes** that can be applied to your slide show.

Try it: Review the Design Ribbon
The Design Ribbon has three groups:
Page Setup
Themes
Background

Keep going, please...

Design ->Themes

Exam 77-883: Microsoft PowerPoint 2010
2. Creating a Slide Presentation
2.4. Format slides.: Apply a Theme

Apply a Theme
Here are the steps to apply a **Theme**.

1. Try it: Select a Theme
Select Slide 1.
Go to **Design->Theme**.
Select a **Theme**: Austin.

What Do You See? The Title Slide was formatted with a Theme. Theme was applied to the color, fonts and layout. This Theme was applied to ALL of the slides in this presentation.

What Else Do You See? The Text Box formatting is still there: patterns, gradients and picture fills.

Keep going...

Design ->Theme

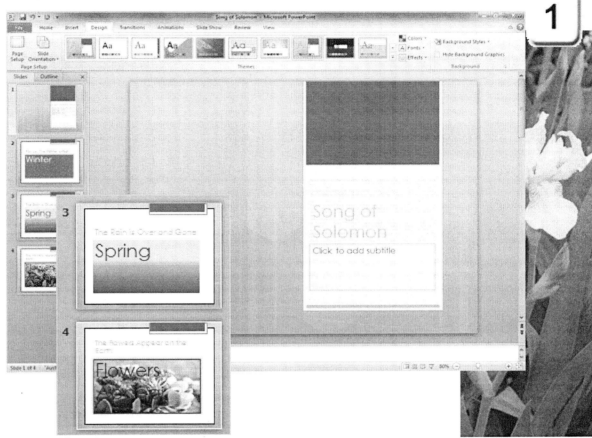

Exam 77-883: Microsoft PowerPoint 2010
2. Creating a Slide Presentation
2.4. Format slides.: Apply a Theme

More Themes

Microsoft PowerPoint has a gallery of **Built In Themes**. The **Design** Ribbon shows the first row in the gallery. Look closely at the scroll bar on the Theme Gallery: the button for **More** is under the arrows.

2. Try it: Find More Themes
Select Slide 1.
Go to **Design->Theme->More**.
Select a Theme: Spring.

What Do You See? This Theme changed the Slide background as well as the Text Box formatting.

Keep going...

Design ->Theme

Exam 77-883: Microsoft PowerPoint 2010
2. Creating a Slide Presentation
2.4. Format slides.: Apply a Theme

Theme Colors

Each Theme comes with a **Color** palette. The colors are applied to the many aspects of the slides including the text and the background colors.

3. Try it: Edit the Theme Color
Still on Slide 1.
Go to **Design->Theme->Colors**.
Select the **Colors**: Metro.

Keep going...

Memo to Self: These are the same Theme Colors that you find in Word and Excel. Using a Theme makes it easy to make your work match each other.

Design ->Theme->Colors

Exam 77-883: Microsoft PowerPoint 2010
2. Creating a Slide Presentation
2.4. Format slides.: Edit the Theme Color

Custom New Theme Colors

If you go to **Create a New Theme**, you get a better idea what the little Color Palette means.

4. Try it: Create a New Theme Colors
Select Slide 1.
Go to **Design->Theme->Colors**.
Select **Create New Theme Colors**.

What Do You See? You will be prompted to edit the Theme Colors for the Accents, links and **Text/Background**.

n this example **Text/Background-Light2** and **Text/Background-Dark2** have been changed to light and dark green.

Click **SAVE** to keep your changes.

Design ->Theme->Colors->Create New Theme Colors

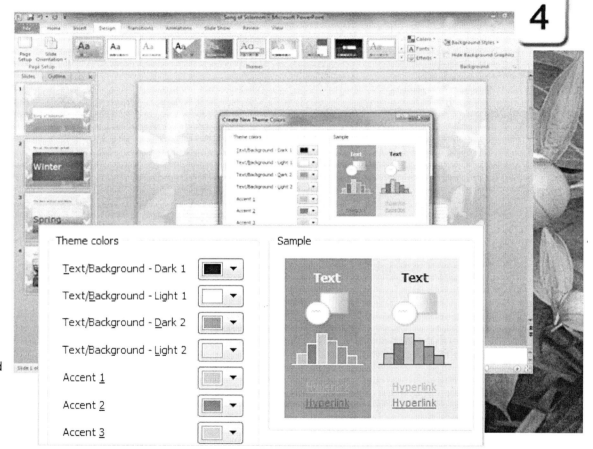

Exam 77-883: Microsoft PowerPoint 2010
2. Creating a Slide Presentation
2.4. Format slides.: Edit the Theme Colors

Theme Fonts

The Theme formats the Titles as well as the Text boxes. The Font formatting is applied to the typeface, size, color and paragraph.

5. Try it: Edit the Theme Font
Select Slide 3.
Go to **Design->Theme->Font**.
Select: Angles.

What Do You See? The Title will be formatted Franklin Gothic Medium, 32 pt. The Text will be formatted Franklin Gothic Book. It is still 96 pt, the custom size we selected earlier. Keep going...

Design ->Theme->Font

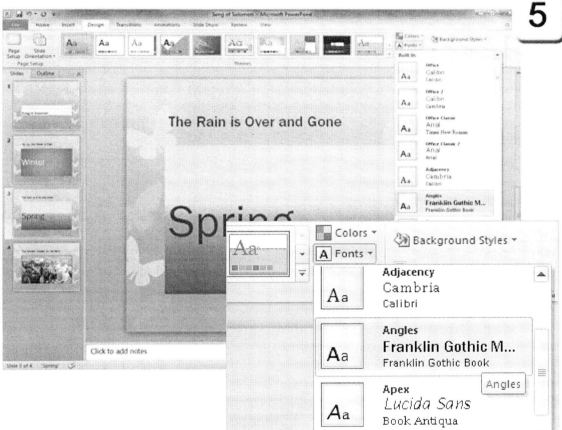

Exam 77-883: Microsoft PowerPoint 2010
2. Creating a Slide Presentation
2.4. Format slides.: Edit the Theme Font

Fix the Font Formatting

Sometimes you need to step back from the **Themes** and look at the results: how does this Theme work with your designs? Do you need to make any improvements?

6. Try it: Format the Font
Select Slide 4.
Select the words: Flowers Appear.
Go to **Home ->Font->Color**.
Select: White
Go to **Home ->Font->Bold.**

What Do You Think? Is the text easier to read? Ok. Let's keep going...

Background Styles

The **Background Styles** lets you choose from a solid Fill Color or a Gradient.

7. Try it: Select a Background Style
Select Slide 3.
Go to **Design ->Background.**
Go to **Background Styles**
Select: Style 8.

What Do You See? The Colors shown in the Background Styles are your Theme Colors. The Background Style was applied to all of the slides in your presentation.

Keep going...one more option.

Design ->Background->Background Styles

Exam 77-883: Microsoft PowerPoint 2010
2. Creating a Slide Presentation
2.4. Format slides.: Edit the Theme Background

Hide Background Graphics

Sometimes it is best to simplify. For example, the Background Style on Slide 4 competes with the picture. Here are the steps to **Hide the Background Graphics**.

8. Try it: Hide Background Graphics
Select Slide 4.
Go to **Design ->Background**.
Check: **Hide Background Graphics.**

What Do You See? This command was applied to the slide that was selected, only.

Really, just one more page...

Design ->Background->Hide Background Graphics

Exam 77-883: Microsoft PowerPoint 2010
2. Creating a Slide Presentation
2.4. Format slides.: Edit the Theme Background

More Background Options
There are **More Background** options as well.

9. Try it: Find More Background Options
Select Slide 4.
Go to **Design ->Background->More**.

What Do You See? The slides Background has the same options as the Text Box:
Solid fill
Gradient fill
Picture or texture fill
Pattern fill

There is an option to Hide background graphics. You can also choose **Apply to All** if you wish.

Very good.

Design ->Background->More

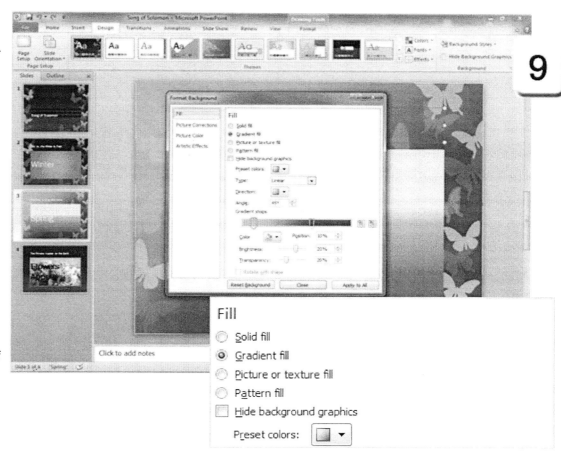

Exam 77-883: Microsoft PowerPoint 2010
2. Creating a Slide Presentation
2.4. Format slides.: Edit the Theme Background

Text Boxes and Themes

This discussion began with a simple Text Box. A Text Box is a Shape that can be edited with the Drawing Tools. We started with Quick Styles and worked our way through the Fill, Outline and Effects. We also looked at the same options in the Design Themes.

Well, this is a good place to take a break.

Try it: Save Your Presentation
1. Go to **File->Save**.
2. Browse to your Documents folder.
3. Fill in the blanks
File Name: Song of Solomon.
Save As Type: PowerPoint Presentation.
Click **SAVE**.

Allez, Allez in Free.
You done real good.
You can get two cookies.

Practice Activities

Lesson 4: Working with Text Boxes

Try This: Do the following steps

1. Open the sample presentation: Do You Have One?
2. Apply the Theme Slipstream. Change the Theme font to Essential
3. Select the content text box on slide 2.
   a. Apply Quick Style Light 1
   b. Outline Colored Fill Turquoise Accent 2.
4. Select the content text box on slide 3.
   a. Apply Quick Style 6 from Other Theme Fills.
   b. Also apply the shape effect Bevel—Cool Slant.
5. Select the content text box on slide 4.
   a. Apply the fill texture Granite.
   b. Format the font to be 24 and Bold.
6. Select the content text box on slide 5.
   a. Format the fill to be Gradient Fill, Light—Linear Left.
   b. Apply Shape Outline Blue, 3pt Weight, Square Dot
7. Select the content text box on slide 6.
   a. Apply a picture fill with a picture from your computer.
   b. If necessary, adjust the font for easier reading
   c. Apply shape effect 3D Isometric Top Up
8. Select the content text box on slide 7. Hide background graphics.
9. Format slide 8, 9, and 10 using shape fills, weights, styles, and effects of your choice.
10. Save this file as Beginning PowerPoint Practice Activity 3

Test Yourself

1. The Home Ribbon has commands for formatting Shapes.
a. True
b. False
Tip: Beginning PowerPoint, page 90

2. Which of the following are formatted when Quick Styles are applied to a shape? (Give all correct answers)
a. Shape Fill
b. Outline
c. Effects
Tip: Beginning PowerPoint, page 91

3. Shape Fill can be which of the following? (Give all correct answers)
a. Color
b. Picture
c. Gradient
d. Texture
Tip: Beginning PowerPoint, page 94

4. Which is true about Gradient? (Give all correct answers)
a. Refers to the gradual change in the intensity of a color
b. Every aspect of a gradient can be edited
Tip: Beginning PowerPoint, page 96, 98

5. Which of the following are options for Shape Outline?
(Give all correct answers)
a. Color
b. Weight
c. Style
Tip: Beginning PowerPoint, page 102

6. Which is a Shape Effect
(Give all correct answers)
a. Shadow
b. Reflection
c. Glow
d. Soft Edges
e. Bevel
f. 3D Rotation
Tip: Beginning PowerPoint, page 104

7. Themes are on which Ribbon?
a. Home
b. Format
c. Design
Tip: Beginning PowerPoint, page 110

8. You can create a custom Theme.
a. True
b. False
Tip: Beginning PowerPoint, page 114

9. The command on the Ribbon to hide background graphics is applied to which of the following?
(Give all correct answers)
a. all slides
b. no slides
c. only the selected slide
Tip: Beginning PowerPoint, page 118

10. When a picture is used as a shape fill, the text automatically adjusts color to be easily read.
a. True
b. False
Tip: Beginning PowerPoint, page 101

PowerPoint 2010: Working with Graphics
Picture, Picture!

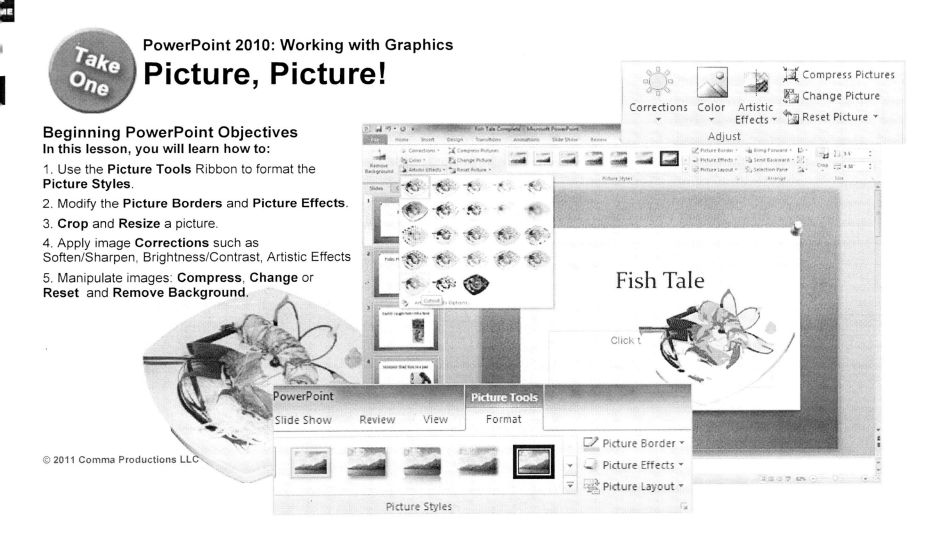

Beginning PowerPoint Objectives
In this lesson, you will learn how to:

1. Use the **Picture Tools** Ribbon to format the **Picture Styles**.

2. Modify the **Picture Borders** and **Picture Effects**.

3. **Crop** and **Resize** a picture.

4. Apply image **Corrections** such as Soften/Sharpen, Brightness/Contrast, Artistic Effects

5. Manipulate images: **Compress**, **Change** or **Reset** and **Remove Background**.

Lesson 5 : Picture, Picture!

1. Readings
Read Lesson 5 in the PowerPoint guide, page 124-152.

Project
A PowerPoint slide show that uses pictures to tell the story.

Downloads
Fishy1.gif
Fishy2.gif
Fishy3.gif
Fishy4.gif
Sushi1.gif
Sushi2.gif
Fish Tale Complete.pptx
Stopping By Woods on a Snowy Evening.pptx

2. Practice
Do the Practice Activity on page 153.

3. Assessment
Review the Test questions on page 154.

Picture Tools->Format

Picture Tools->Format

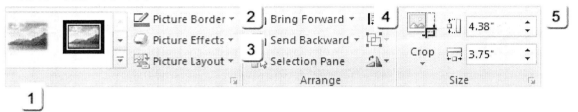

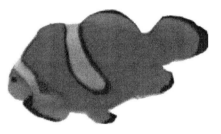

Menu Maps
From the **Picture Tools->Format Ribbon**.
1. Picture Tools->Format->Picture Styles, page 135
2. Picture Tools->Format->Picture Styles-> Picture Border, page 137
3. Picture Tools->Format->Picture Styles-> Picture Effects, page 138
4. Picture Tools->Format-> Size->Crop, page 140
5. Picture Tools->Format-> Size, page 141
6. Picture Tools->Format-> Adjust->Corrections, page 144
7. Picture Tools->Format-> Adjust->Color, page 146
8. Picture Tools->Format-> Adjust->Artistic Effects, page 147
9. Picture Tools->Format-> Adjust->Remove Background, page 152

Every Picture Tells a Story

PowerPoint is to Pictures as Word is to Text. The images and pictures in a presentation make a connection with the audience. Having an emotional connection is one of the key elements that makes a message--or website--sticky. Technical terms: "Sticky" means that people want to stick around. This lesson introduces the Picture Tools and the options for working with your pictures: Styles, Size, and Adjustments.

Start -> All Programs ->Microsoft Office-> Microsoft Office PowerPoint 2010

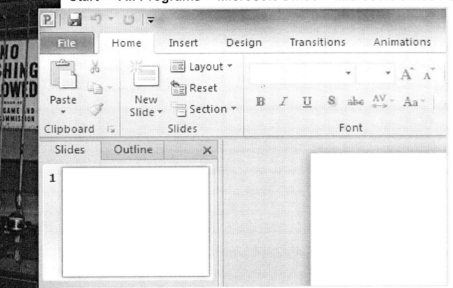

Please Start Microsoft PowerPoint
What do you see at the top of the screen?
Is there a Title Bar that says Microsoft PowerPoint? Yes.

Is there a **Home** Ribbon with the Clipboard, Font and Paragraph Groups? Yes.

If your screen looks similar to the example on this page, then you are ready to get started.

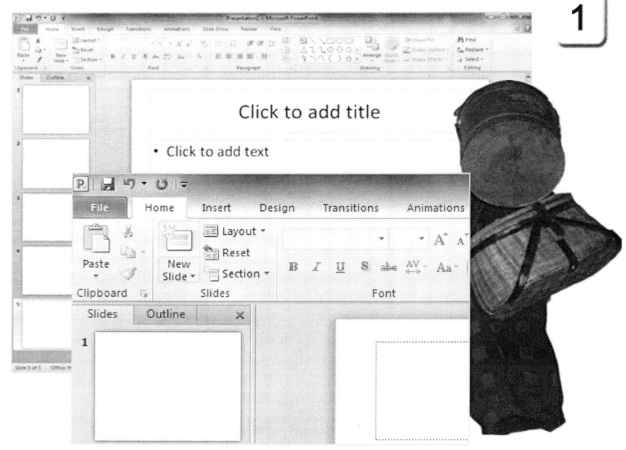

Before You Begin

This lesson will go through the **Picture** tools. The Picture tools include Quick Styles, Shape Fill, Shape Outline, and Shape Effects. We will also look at the PowerPoint **Themes**.

1. Try it: Create a New Presentation
Open PowerPoint. You should see a new, blank presentation.
Go to **Home ->Slides->New Slide**
Please add four new slides.

Keep going...

Memo to Self: You do not have to MATCH the images and special effects shown on these pages.

Please add your own pictures if you wish. It is more important that you begin with something and try the options that are available.

Enter the Titles

2. Try it: Add Text to the Titles

Slide 1, type: A Fish Tale
Slide 2, type: Fishy, Fishy in the brook.
Slide 3, type: Daddy caught him with a hook.
Slide 4, type: Mommy cooked him in a pan.
Slide 5, type: Baby ate them like a man.

Keep going...!

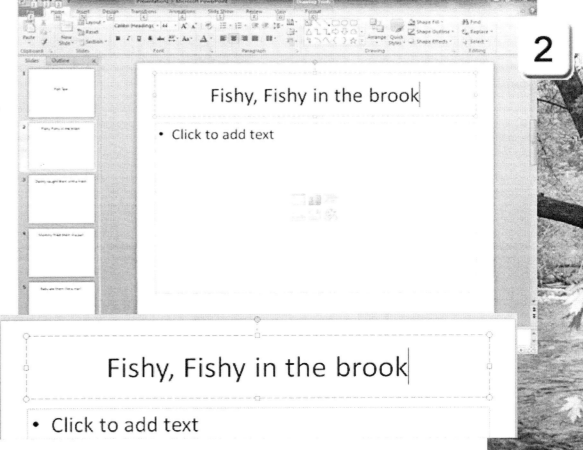

Exam 77-883: Microsoft PowerPoint 2010
2. Creating a Slide Presentation
2.5. Enter and format text

Choose a Theme
3. Try it: Apply a Theme
Go to **Design ->Themes**.
Select a Theme: Pushpin.

What Do You See? The **Theme** was applied to the Text (Font, Color, Size), Textbox and Slide formatting. The slides have a background graphic. The Theme was applied to all of the slides in this presentation.

Keep going...

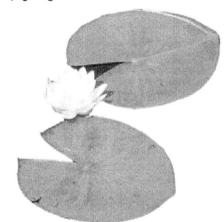

Design ->Themes

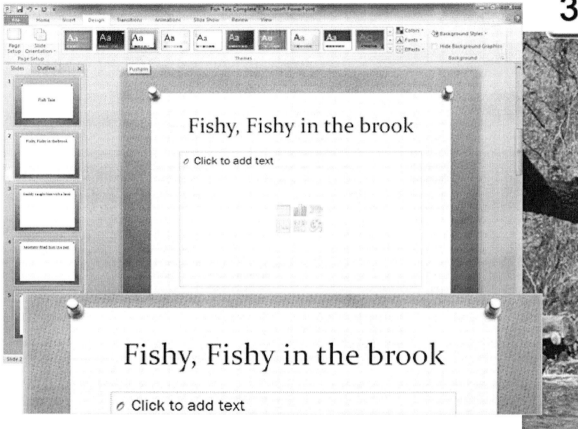

Exam 77-883: Microsoft PowerPoint 2010
2. Creating a Slide Presentation
2.4. Format slides: Apply a Theme

Change the Slide Layout

By default, the slides have one Text Box. Say you wanted to split the Text Box so you could have a bulleted list on the left side and a picture on the right.

You can use the **Home Ribbon** to change the **Slide Layout**.

4. Try it: Change the Slide Layout
We are still on Slide 2.
Go to **Home ->Slides->Layout**.
Select: Two Content.

Keep going...

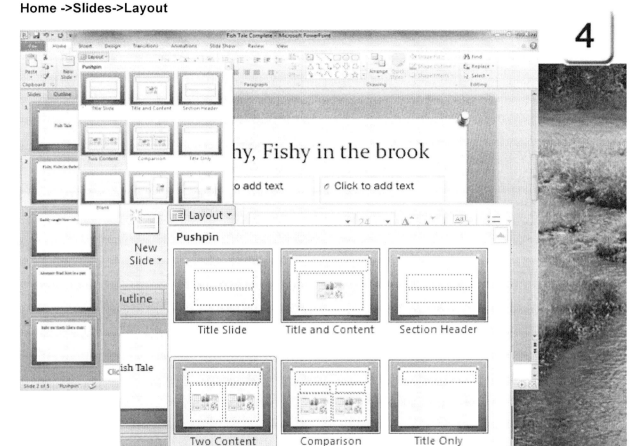

Exam 77-883: Microsoft PowerPoint 2010
2. Creating a Slide Presentation
2.4. Format slides: Change the Slide Layout

Side by SIde Content

5. What Do You See? The Text Box has two Placeholders. Both Placeholders have the little options to add content, so either Placeholder could display text, picture, chart or media.

Try This, Too: Change the Other Slides
Select Slides 3, 4, and 5.
Go to **Home ->Slides->Layout.**
Select: Two Content.

So far so good. These pages set up the presentation with Text, Theme and Layout. Now, if you are ready, it is finally time to work with **PICTURES**!

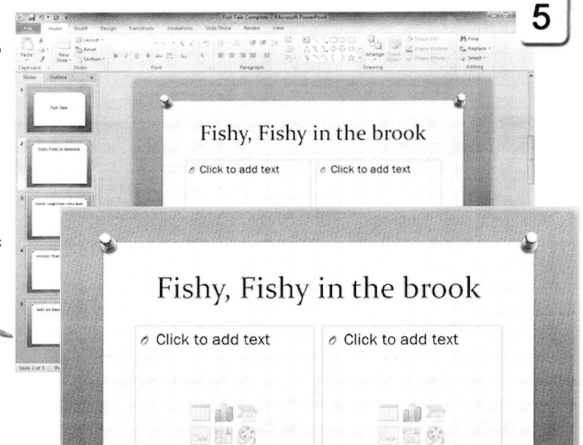

Exam 77-883: Microsoft PowerPoint 2010
2. Creating a Slide Presentation
2.4. Format slides: Change the Slide Layout

Find the Placeholder

If you look in the center of the bottom Text Box you should see a **Placeholder.** This Placeholder has little buttons that let you add a Table, Chart, SmartArt, Picture, ClipArt or Media clip (sound or video).

6. Try it: Find the Placeholder
Select Slide 2.

What Do You See? When you run your mouse over the buttons in the Placeholder, you will see a **Tool Tip** that says what this button will add.

Keep going...

Design ->Page Setup

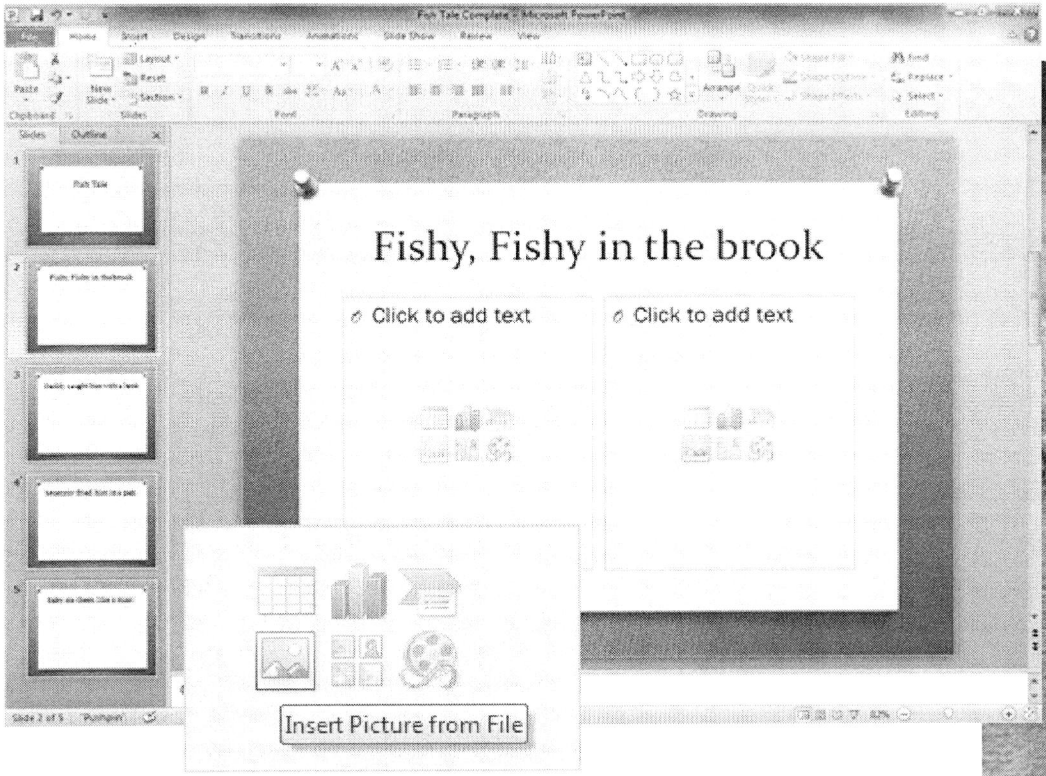

6

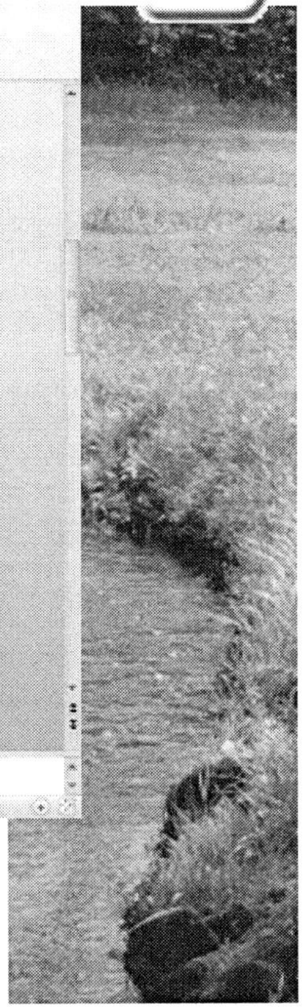

Exam 77-883: Microsoft PowerPoint 2010
2. Creating a Slide Presentation
2.5. Enter and format text: Use a Placeholder

Insert ->Illustrations->Picture

Insert Pictures

This slide show will have a different picture on each slide. There are four sample pictures that you can download. You can also use your own pictures if you wish.

1. Try it: Insert Picture
Go to Slide 2: Fishy, Fishy in a brook.
You should see two Placeholders.
Go to the right **Placeholder**.
Click on: **Insert Picture from File.**

Browse to your Documents folder.
Select: Fishy1.gif
Click on **Insert** and keep going...

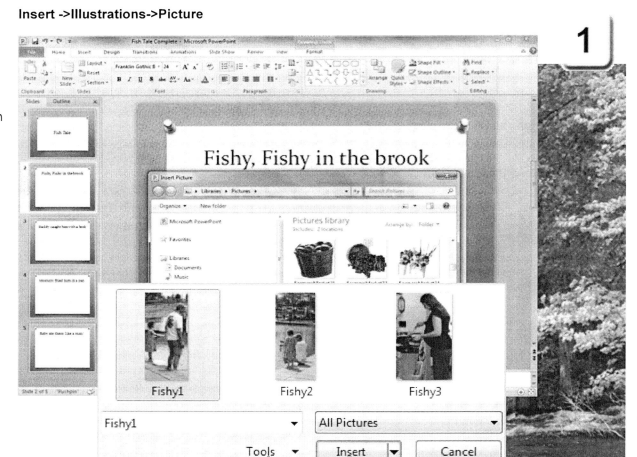

Exam 77-883: Microsoft PowerPoint 2010
3. Working with Graphical and Multimedia Elements
3.2. Manipulate images: Insert Illustrations

Insert More Pictures

Each slide should have a picture in the right Placeholder.

2. Try it: Insert More Pictures
Go to Slide 3: Daddy caught him...
Go to the right Placeholder.
Click on: **Insert Picture from File**.
Browse to your Documents folder.
Select: Fishy2.gif

Go to Slide 4: Mommy cooked him...
Go to the right Placeholder.
Click on: **Insert Picture from File**.
Browse to your Documents folder.
Select: Fishy3.gif

Go to Slide 5: Baby ate them...
Go to the right Placeholder.
Click on: **Insert Picture from File**.
Browse to your Documents folder.
Select: Fishy4.gif

Keep going...

Insert ->Illustrations->Picture

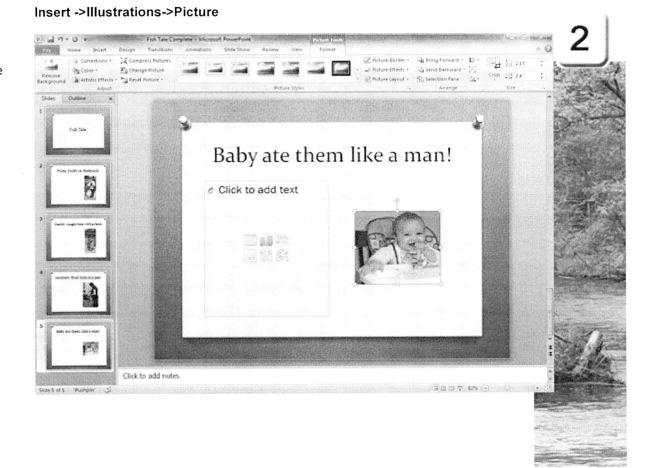

Exam 77-883: Microsoft PowerPoint 2010
3. Working with Graphical and Multimedia Elements
3.2. Manipulate images: Insert Illustrations

Hello, Picture Tools!

When you click on a picture, you will see the picture frame and handles. That is your clue that the picture has been selected.

You should also see the **Picture Tools.** The Picture Tools appear when you click on a picture. They disappear when the picture is no longer selected.

3. Try it: Now You See It, Now You Don't. Click on the picture. The Picture Tools are available. Click on the blank page so that the picture in not selected (it no longer has handles) and the Picture Tools hide.

Memo to Self: The Picture Tools always appear on the far right side of the Ribbons. Sometimes, you need to look. PowerPoint may still display the last Ribbon you touched, say the Home Ribbon, even though you just selected a picture.

Picture Tools->Format

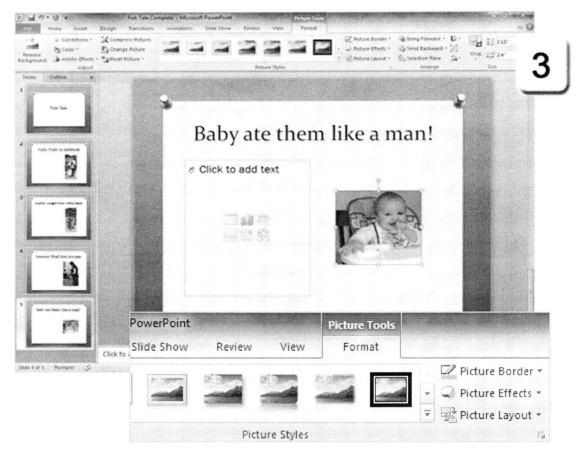

Exam 77-883: Microsoft PowerPoint 2010
3. Working with Graphical and Multimedia Elements
3.2. Manipulate images: Format Illustrations

Picture Styles

Microsoft PowerPoint 2007 and 2010 have a rich library of **Picture Styles**. The Styles format the **Picture Border** and the **Picture Effects**.

1. Try it: Format the Picture Style
Begin on Slide 5. Select the picture.
Go to **Picture Tools->Format.**
Go to **Picture Styles.**
Click on **Drop Shadow Rectangle.**

2. What Do You See? The **Style** added a thin border and a shadow to the picture. Keep going...

Exam 77-883: Microsoft PowerPoint 2010
3. Working with Graphical and Multimedia Elements
3.2. Manipulate images: Apply Styles

More Picture Styles

The Picture Tools show only one row of the **Picture Styles** library. Look carfeully at the scroll bar on the right side. There are three buttons on the Picture Styles scroll bar: Up, Down, and More.

3. Try it: Find More Picture Styles
The picture on Slide 5 is selected.
Go to **Picture Tools->Format.**
Go to **Picture Styles.**
Click on the down arrow for **More.**

Picture Styles

What Do You See? Should see several more rows of Styles. The example on this page is Perspective Shadow, White.

So far, so good.

Picture Tools->Format->Picture Styles

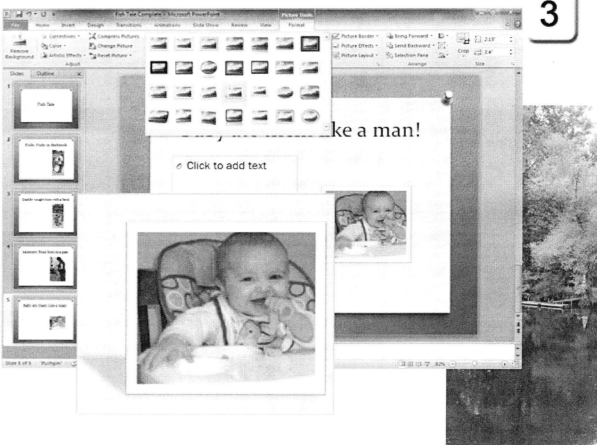

Exam 77-883: Microsoft PowerPoint 2010
3. Working with Graphical and Multimedia Elements
3.2. Manipulate images: Apply Styles

Format the Picture Border

You can create your own Picture Style. Let's begin with the Picture Border. There are several options you can edit including Color, Weight and Dashes.

1. Try it: Format the Picture Border
Go to Slide 2. Select the picture.
Go to **Picture Tools->Format.**
Go to **Picture Styles-> Picture Border.**
Select the **Color**: Black
Select the **Weight**: 3 pt

2. What Do You See? The Border menu offers the **Theme Colors** as well as the Standard Colors.

The **Weight** and **Dashes** menus show a short list of formats. There are **More** options at the bottom of these lists.

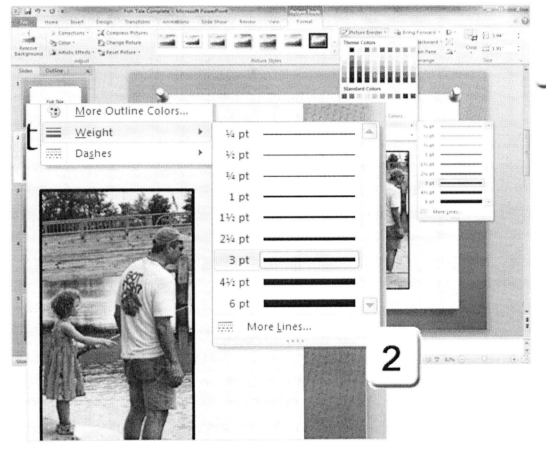

Exam 77-883: Microsoft PowerPoint 2010
3. Working with Graphical and Multimedia Elements
3.2. Manipulate images: Edit the Border Styles

Add Picture Effects

The **Picture Effects** include:
Preset (Built in Styles)
Shadow
Reflection
Glow
Soft Edges
Bevel
3-D Rotation.

1. Try it: Add Picture Effects

Still on Slide 2. The picture is selected.
Go to **Picture Tools->Format.**
Go to **Picture Styles-> Picture Effects.**
Go to **Shadow.**
Click on **Perspective.**

Where Have You Seen This Before?

These are the same Picture Effects that
you can apply to a Shape or a Text Box.

Picture Tools->Format->Picture Styles-> Picture Effects

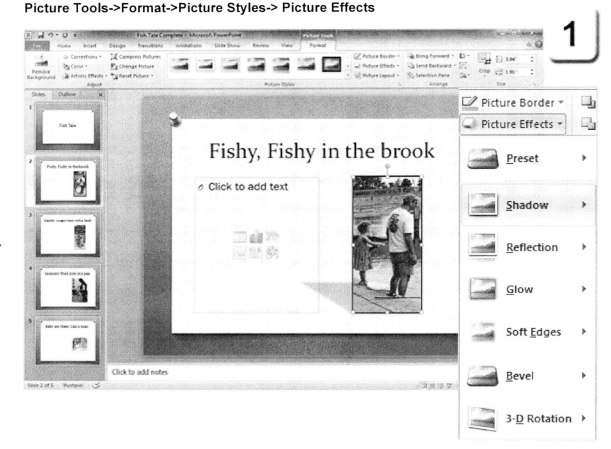

Exam 77-883: Microsoft PowerPoint 2010
3. Working with Graphical and Multimedia Elements
3.2. Manipulate images: Add Picture Effects

More Picture Effects

The **Preset** formats add more than one Picture Effect for unusual results.

2. Try it: Add a Preset Picture Effect
Go to Slide 3. Select the picture.
Go to **Picture Tools->Format.**
Go to **Picture Styles-> Picture Effects**.
Go to **Preset 4**.

What Do You See? The Picture Effect added a Shadow and a Bevel. The Borders were formatted as well.

Very good.

Exam 77-883: Microsoft PowerPoint 2010
3. Working with Graphical and Multimedia Elements
3.2. Manipulate images: Add Picture Effects

Crop the Image

If you look at the sample image for Slide 4 you probably noticed that there is a date time stamp. You can **Crop** the picture to remove part of the image. Look in the **Picture Tools** for the **Crop** button. It is part of the **Size** group.

1. Try it: Crop the Image
Go to Slide 4 and select the picture.
Go to **Picture Tools->Format-> Size**.
Click on **Crop**.

2. What Do You See? When you click on **Crop** the picture will have a new frame. **Crop Marks** are available in each corner and on all of the sides. You can drag the bottom Crop Mark up until the date/time stamp is no longer visible.

Click on **Crop** again and the edits will be saved.

Good Question: Is the image cut permanently? No. Say you saved this presentation and opened it later. When you click on the cropped image, you will see the bottom portion that is in grey is still available...unless you **Compress** all Pictures and tell PowerPoint to delete the cropped area.

Picture Tools->Format-> Size->Crop

Exam 77-883: Microsoft PowerPoint 2010
3. Working with Graphical and Multimedia Elements
3.2. Manipulate images: Crop an image

Change the Image Size
You may wish to **Resize** your picture after you Crop it. Here are the steps.

3. Try it: Resize the Picture
The picture on Slide 4 is selected and the Picture Tools are available.

Go to **Picture Tools->Format-> Size**.
Change the **Height**: 4
Hit the **ENTER** key on your keyboard.

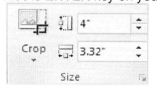

What Do You See? The **Width** resized **automatically** to be the right proportions.

Keep going...

Picture Tools->Format-> Size

Exam 77-883: Microsoft PowerPoint 2010
3. Working with Graphical and Multimedia Elements
3.2. Manipulate images: Resize a Picture

Crop to Shape

The **Crop** button has a very interesting option. You can use this button to change the Picture Shape.

4. Try it: Crop to Shape
The picture on Slide 4 is selected.
Go to the **Picture Tools->Format-> Size.**
Go to **Crop to Shape.**
Select: **Rounded Rectangle.**

What Do You See? The picture should have in new shape with rounded corners.

That was alright, on a scale of 1 to 10.

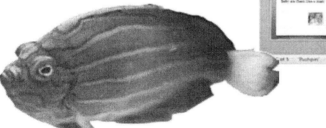

Exam 77-883: Microsoft PowerPoint 2010
3. Working with Graphical and Multimedia Elements
3.2. Manipulate images: Crop to Shape

Apply Image Corrections

Every picture tells a story, but not every picture is "picture perfect." Microsoft PowerPoint has several tools you can use to **Adjust** the image.

1. Before You Begin: Insert a Picture
Go to Slide 1.
Go to **Insert ->Picture**.
Browse to your Documents folder for the sample picture, Sushi1.gif.
Click **Insert** to add this picture to Slide 1.

Still Before You Begin: Move the Title Box
Select the Title Box on Slide 1.
Drag the Text Box so that the words do not overlap the picture.

Keep going, please.

Insert ->Picture

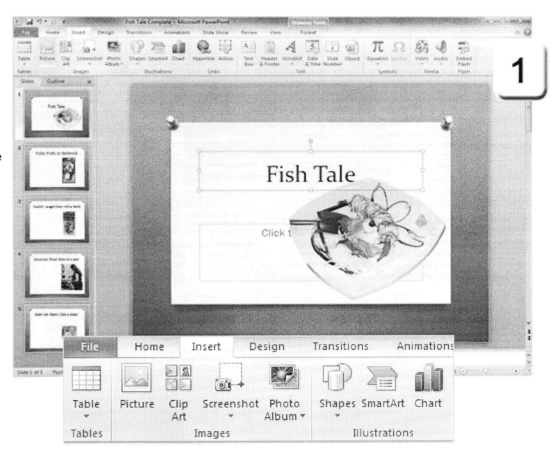

Exam 77-883: Microsoft PowerPoint 2010
3. Working with Graphical and Multimedia Elements
3.2. Manipulate images: Apply image corrections-Brightness and Contrast

Adjust: Brightness and Contrast

Brightness is the amount of light on the subject.
Contrast is the difference between absolute white and absolute black, Changing the Brightness can make an image much more alive and colorful.

2. Try it: Adjust the Brightness and Contrast
Go to Slide 1 and select the picture. The Picture Tools should be available.

Go to **Picture Tools->Format-> Adjust**.
Go to **Corrections->Brightness and Contrast**.
Select: Brightness: 0% (Normal) Contrast: +40%.

What Do You See? There are three different Picture Correction options:
Sharpen and Soften
Brightness and Contrast
Picture Corrections Options.

Each little square in the library is a different percentage of Brightness or Contrast. When you run your cursor over the Correction, you should see a Live Preview of the results.

Keep going...

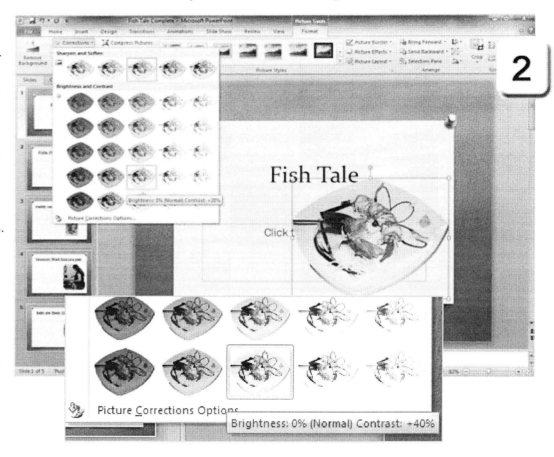

Exam 77-883: Microsoft PowerPoint 2010
3. Working with Graphical and Multimedia Elements
3.2. Manipulate images: Apply image corrections-Brightness and Contrast

Adjust: Sharpen and Soften

When you **Sharpen** an image, you make the edges more pronounced. When you **Soften** an image, you feather the edges and the image may be more blurry.

3. Try it: Sharpen the Image
Go to **Picture Tools->Format-> Adjust.**
Go to **Sharpen and Soften.**
Select: Sharpen 50%.

Keep going. There are more Adjustments...

Where Have You Seen This Before? A Wedding Vignette is a picture of two hands wearing wedding rings. It is usually very soft focus.

Exam 77-883: Microsoft PowerPoint 2010
3. Working with Graphical and Multimedia Elements
3.2. Manipulate images: Apply image corrections-Sharpen and Soften

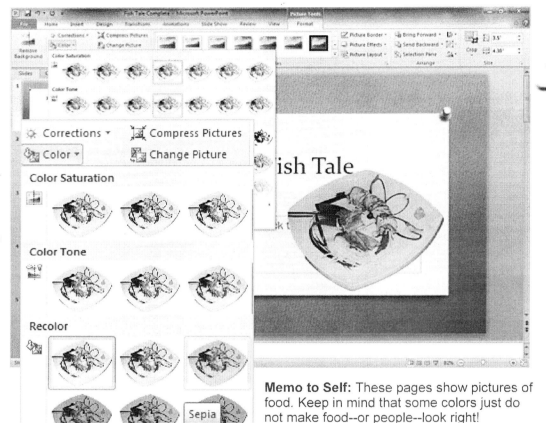

Adjust: Color

Color can convey good will (sky blue) or trust (warm brown). Let's look at the options for adjusting the Picture Color.

4. Try it: Adjust the Color
Go to **Picture Tools->Format-> Adjust.**
Go to **Color->Recolor.**
Select: Sepia.

What Do You See? There are three Color options that you can adjust including:

Color Saturation adds or removes the color. 0% creates a black and white image and 400% blasts the image with color like a poster.

Color Tone adds red to make a picture warmer and blue to cool it down. Blue is also used to remove the yellow tone that comes from indoor lighting.

Recolor adds a color filter on the image.

Please **UNDO** the **Color** and continue.

Picture Tools->Format-> Adjust->Color-> Recolor

Memo to Self: These pages show pictures of food. Keep in mind that some colors just do not make food--or people--look right!

Exam 77-883: Microsoft PowerPoint 2010
3. Working with Graphical and Multimedia Elements
3.2. Manipulate images: Apply image corrections-Color

Adjust: Artistic Effects
The next example falls under the topic "You gotta see this." **Artistic Effects** add a Filter to your image.

5. Try it: Add an Artistic Effect
Go to **Picture Tools->Format-> Adjust.**
Go to **Artistic Effects.**
Select: **Cutout**.

What Do You See? The options include pencil strokes, paint brush, water color sponge, grain, screens and glowing edges.

Yes. That was worth investigating.

Exam 77-883: Microsoft PowerPoint 2010
3. Working with Graphical and Multimedia Elements
3.2. Manipulate images: Apply image corrections-Artistic Effects

Adjust: Compress Pictures

PowerPoint is a visual platform. A simple slide show may have many pictures. There is an option to **Compress** the pictures, to reduce the size of the presentation.

6. Try it: Compress the Pictures
Begin on Slide 1. Select the picture.
Go to **Picture Tools->Format-> Adjust**.
Select **Compress Pictures.**

What Do You See? You will be prompted to choose what resolution you wish. The Target output for Print resolution is higher than Screen or E-mail. It is a compromise between size and clarity.

What Else Do You See? You can **Compress** just the picture you selected or all of the pictures in this presentation.

This is also where you can **Delete cropped areas of pictures.**

Click **OK** and keep going...

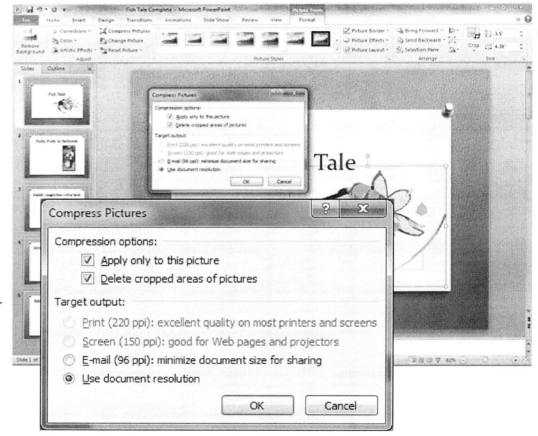

Exam 77-883: Microsoft PowerPoint 2010
3. Working with Graphical and Multimedia Elements
3.2. Manipulate images: Apply image corrections-Compress Pictures

Adjust: Change Picture

Say you formatted a picture with several Styles and Adjustments. Say you decided that a different picture would work better.

Is there a way to **Change** the Picture? What happens to the picture formatting?

7. Try it: Change the Picture
Go to Slide 1 and select the picture. The Picture Tools should be available.

Go to **Picture Tools->Format-> Adjust**. Select: **Change Picture.**

You will be prompted to **Browse** for a picture. The example on these pages is the Sushi2.gif, however you can use a different picture if you wish.

Keep going...

Memo to Self: You can also right-click the image to go to **Change Picture**.

Picture Tools->Format-> Adjust->Change Picture

Exam 77-883: Microsoft PowerPoint 2010
3. Working with Graphical and Multimedia Elements
3.2. Manipulate images: Apply image corrections-Change Picture

Change Picture, continued

What Do You See? Change Picture replaces the previous picture with a new one. However, the new image may or may not inherit the previous picture's custom formatting.

Go Ahead: Format the Picture
Select the replacement picture.
The Picture Tools should be available.
Select a Style.
Select a Picture Effect.
Select a Color.

Keep going...

Exam 77-883: Microsoft PowerPoint 2010
3. Working with Graphical and Multimedia Elements
3.2. Manipulate images: Apply image corrections-Change Picture

Adjust: Reset Picture

What if all of these Picture Styles, Effects and adjustments don't work out very well? Is there a better way to go back to the original, other than a hundred Undos? Yes.

8. Try it: Reset the Picture
Select the formatted picture.
Go to **Picture Tools->Format.**
Go to **Adjust-> Reset Picture**.

You can **Reset** just the Picture, or the Picture and the Size.

Picture Tools->Format-> Adjust->Reset Picture

Exam 77-883: Microsoft PowerPoint 2010
3. Working with Graphical and Multimedia Elements
3.2. Manipulate images: Apply image corrections-Reset Picture

More Adjustments: Remove Background

You can use the Picture Tools to **Remove the Background** on an image. This is a new option in PowerPoint 2007 and 2010. The Computer Mama sez this option works rather well.

1. Try it: Remove the Background
Begin on Slide 5. Select the picture.
Go to **Picture Tools->Format-> Adjust**.
Select **Remove Background.**

Keep going...

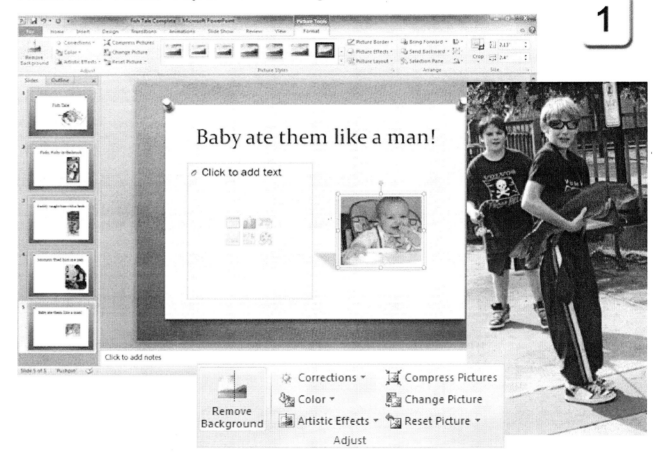

Exam 77-883: Microsoft PowerPoint 2010
3. Working with Graphical and Multimedia Elements
3.2. Manipulate images: Apply image corrections-Remove Background

Remove Background

2. Mark the Areas

Microsoft PowerPoint 2010 compares the colors in the image and makes a reasonable guess. The suggested background is displayed in a pink mask. The areas that will be kept are shown in full color.

3. Edit the Marks

Look carefully at your picture. In this example, I noticed that some of the areas around the edge of the chair needed to be marked **Areas to Keep**. Others needed to be marked **Remove**.

4. Keep the Changes

When you click on **Keep Changes**, you will see your picture without the background. You can change your Marked Areas by clicking again on Remove Background. Your background marks will still be there if you wish to add or remove some areas.

Picture Tools->Format-> Adjust->Remove Background

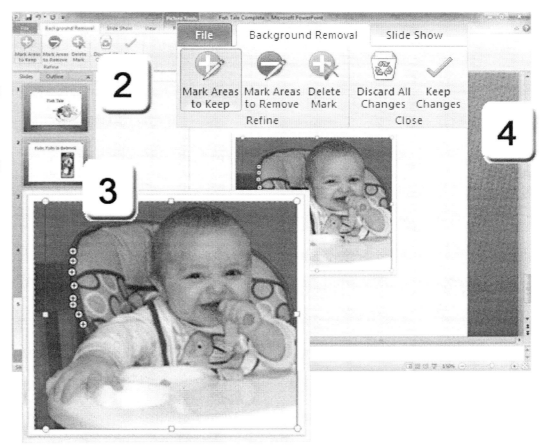

Exam 77-883: Microsoft PowerPoint 2010
3. Working with Graphical and Multimedia Elements
3.2. Manipulate images: Apply image corrections-Remove Background

The Picture Tools

Try This: Save your Presentation
Go to **File->Save**.
Browse to your Documents folder.
Name the file: Fish Tale.pptx.
Click on **Save**.

Summary
This discussion introduced the Picture Tools.
We began with the Picture Styles, then
practiced how to crate our own custom Styles
by formatting the Picture Border and Picture
Effects.

We also investigated the various way we can
Adjust a Picture for Brightness, Contrast, Color
and Compression.

Well, you done good.
You get a cookie.

Practice Activities

Lesson 5: Working with Pictures

Try This: Do the following steps

1. Open the file Stopping By the Woods on a Snowy Evening.pptx
2. Apply the Theme Metro
3. On the title slide, insert a picture from your computer. Apply picture Effect: Reflected Rounded Rectangle
4. On slide 2, resize the photo to be 4 inches tall.
a. Use the remove background tool and accept all changes.
b. Change the slide layout to Title and Content
5. On slide 3, apply the picture Style Soft Oval
6. On slide 4, crop the photo to remove the house visible in the upper left. Apply a white 2 ¼ pt border.
7. On slide 5, adjust the brightness so the picture is darker. Use correction Brightness -40%, Contrast +20%.
8. On slide 6, use the crop to shape tool and select Oval Callout.
a. Apply Artistic Affect Glow Diffused
b. Change the slide layout to Title and Content
9. On slide 7, recolor the picture to Color Tone Temperature 4700K.
a. Apply the soften command Soften 50%.
10. On slide 8, apply Soft Edges 10pt.
a. Apply Glow, color White Text 1
b. Apply 3D rotation Off Axis 1 Left
11. Compress all pictures and remove cropped areas.
12. Save this file as Beginning PowerPoint Activity 4

Test Yourself

1. Which of the following does Theme apply to? (Give all correct answers)
a. Text Color
b. Text Size
c. Text Box
d. Slide Formatting
Tip: Beginning PowerPoint, page 128

2. Which are Slide Layout Options? (Give all correct answers)
a. Title and Content
b. Two Content
c. Comparison
d. Title Slide
Tip: Beginning PowerPoint, page 129

3. How are the Picture Tools Ribbon accessed?
a. Select the picture
b. View--> Picture Tools
c. File--> View--> Picture Tools
Tip: Beginning PowerPoint, page 134

4. Which do Picture Styles format? (Give all correct answers)
a. Picture Border
b. Picture Effects
c. Picture Brightness
Tip: Beginning PowerPoint, page 135

5. The only way to add a Picture Border is with Styles.
a. True
b. False
Tip: Beginning PowerPoint, page 137

6. Which are Picture Effects? (Give all correct answers)
a. Shadow
b. Reflection
c. Soft Edges
d. 3D Rotation
Tip: Beginning PowerPoint, page 138

7. Which is true? (Give all correct answers)
a. When you sharpen an image, you make the edges more pronounced
b. When you soften an image, the edges are feathered and more blurry
Tip: Beginning PowerPoint, page 145

8. Reset Picture removes any formatting or adjustments, returning the picture to its original format.
a. True
b. False
Tip: Beginning PowerPoint, page 151

9. Which command adjusts the size of a picture to reduce the size of a presentation?
a. Resize
b. Compress
c. Shrink
Tip: Beginning PowerPoint, page 148

10. Which are options for adjusting the color of a picture? (Give all correct answers)
a. Color Saturation
b. Color Tone
c. Recolor
Tip: Beginning PowerPoint, page 146

PowerPoint 2010: Working with Graphics

Shapes and SmartArt

Beginning PowerPoint Objectives
In this lesson, you will learn how to:

1. Control the **AutoCorrect** options for a Placeholder, such as a Text Box.

2. Use the **Design** Ribbon to Promote and Demote bullet levels in a **SmartArt** graphic.

3. Identify and use the **SmartArt Tools** to edit a SmartArt graphic.

4. Change the SmartArt: Add more Shapes, Reorder the Shapes, and change the Layout.

5. **Convert** the SmartArt to Text or Shapes.

© 2011 Comma Productions LLC

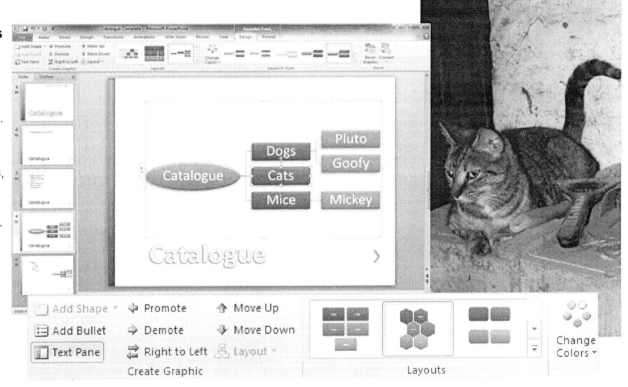

Lesson 6 : Shapes and SmartArt

1. Readings

Read Lesson 6 in the PowerPoint guide, page 157-187.

Project

A presentation that uses **SmartArt** to add interactive graphics.

Downloads

Catalogue Complete.pptx

2. Practice

Do the Practice Activity on page 188.

3. Assessment

Review the Test questions on page 189.

SmartArt->Design Ribbon

SmartArt->Format Ribbon

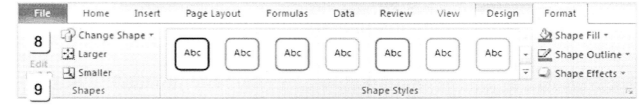

Menu Maps

From the **SmartArt Tools->Design Ribbon**.

1. Design->Create Graphic->Text Pane, page 172
2. Design->Create Graphic->Add Shape, page 174
3. Design->Create Graphic->Promote, page 176
4. Design->Create Graphic->Right to Left, page 177
5. Design-> Layout, page 178
6. Design->SmartArt Styles-> Change Color, page 179
7. Design->SmartArt Styles-> Styles, page 180

More Menu Maps

From the **SmartArt Tools->Format Ribbon**.

8. Format->Shapes->Change Shape, page 182
9. Format->Shapes->Larger, page 183

Shapes and SmartArt

Pictures are one way to tell your story. Shapes and SmartArt are another. Shapes let you visualize concepts. One very useful example of SmartArt is an organization chart. The hierarchy lets you see a different view of a company than you would get from a catalogue of the employee pictures. Shapes and SmartArt use many of the same Drawing tools we played with earlier. This is a fun lesson: enjoy!

Start -> All Programs ->Microsoft Office-> Microsoft Office PowerPoint 2010

Please Start Microsoft PowerPoint
What do you see at the top of the screen? Is there a Title Bar that says Microsoft PowerPoint? Yes.

Is there a **Home** Ribbon with the Clipboard, Font and Paragraph Groups? Yes.

If your screen looks similar to the example on this page, then you are ready to get started.

All barns need a barn cat....keep going

Before You Begin

This lesson starts with some options for managing lots and lots of text in a Text Box. Then, we'll look at **Shapes** and **SmartArt**: two more ways to make a point in your presentation.

1. Try it: Create a New Presentation

Open Microsoft PowerPoint 2010. You should see a new, blank presentation. Go to **Home ->Slides->New Slide** Please add four new slides.

Keep going...

Memo to Self: You do not have to MATCH the images and special effects shown on these pages.

Please add your own pictures if you wish. It is more important that you begin with something and try the options that are available.

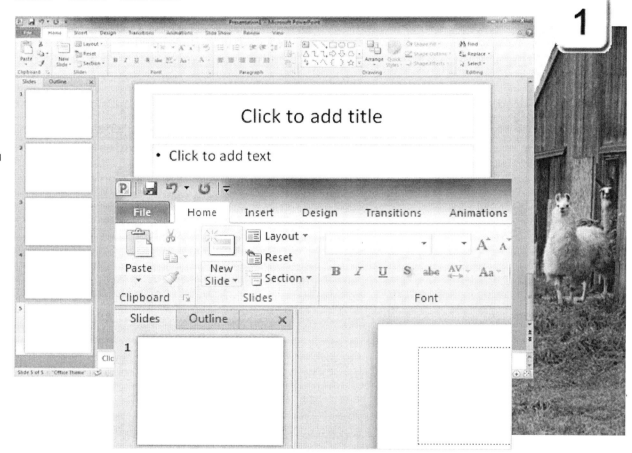

Exam 77-883: Microsoft PowerPoint 2010
2. Creating a Slide Presentation
2.5. Enter and format text

Enter the Titles

2. Try This: Add Text to the Titles
Select Slide 1. Type the following:
Title: Catalogue
Text: Rosalie Moore (B.1910)

Select Slide 2. Type the following:
Title: Catalogue
Text: Cats sleep fat and walk thin.

Select Slide 3. Type the following:
Title: Catalogue
Text: (blank, so far)

Keep going...

Mariellen's barn cat had kittens....keep going

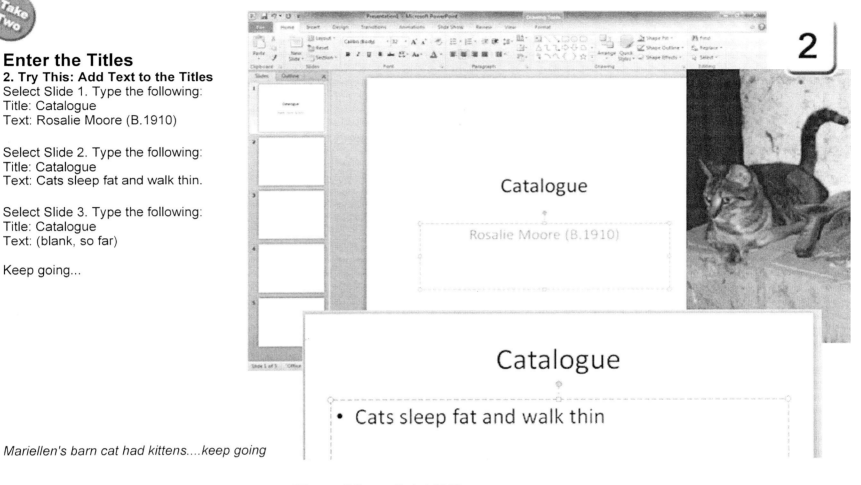

Exam 77-883: Microsoft PowerPoint 2010
2. Creating a Slide Presentation
2.5. Enter and format text

Choose a Theme

3. Try This: Select a Theme
Select Slide 1.
Go to **Design->Themes**.
Select a Theme: Thermal.

Try This, Too: Change the Layout
Select Slide 2.
Go to **Home->Slides-Layout.**
Choose a **Layout**: Two content.
Repeat for Slide 3, 4 and 5.

What Do You See? This step changed the **Slide Layout**. Each slide now has two place holders.

Keep going...

Lots of kittens....keep going

Design ->Themes

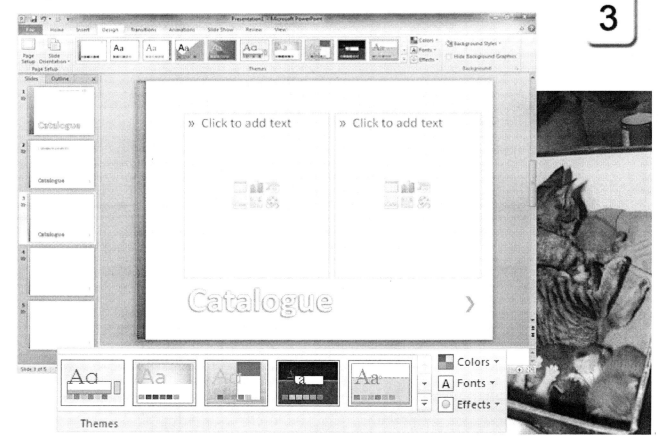

Exam 77-883: Microsoft PowerPoint 2010
2. Creating a Slide Presentation
2.4. Format slides: Apply a Theme

Enter a Lot of Text

4. Try This: Add a Lot of Text

Select Slide 3. Type the following:
Title: Catalogue
Text: Cats, when they sleep, slump: When they walk, pull in-
And where the plump's been, there's skin.

What Do You See? The words in the Text Box wrap: technical term for continues on the next line. When you type ENTER on the keyboard, a new bullet will be added to the list. Keep going...

Lady at 2 weeks old, the only girl in the litter....

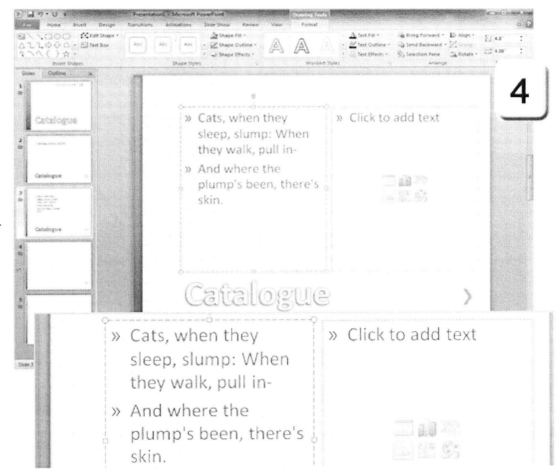

Exam 77-883: Microsoft PowerPoint 2010
2. Creating a Slide Presentation
2.5. Enter and format text

Format the Text

5. Try it: Format the Text
Go to Slide 3.
Select all of the text in the Text Box.
Go to **Home ->Font->Size**
Choose a size: 36 pt

What Do You See? As you increase the Font size there will be a point where the text will be too big and it will not fit on the screen, I know, that's stating the obvious, but keep going...

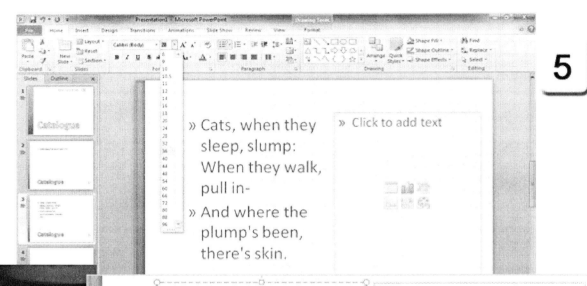

Exam 77-883: Microsoft PowerPoint 2010
2. Creating a Slide Presentation
2.5. Enter and format text: Change text format

Resize the Text Box

Say you resized the Text Box and made it smaller. What happens to the text?

6. Try it: Resize the Text Box
Select the Text Box on Slide 3. The handles will be available. Use any handle and drag until the Text Box is smaller.

What Do You See? Microsoft PowerPoint automatically resized the text so that it would fit. The Font size in this example was downsized from 36 pt to 28 pt.

What Else Do You See? Look for a little button with two arrows. This is the **AutoFit Options.** When you click on AutoFit, you should see:
AutoFit Text to Placeholder
Stop Fitting Text to This Placeholder,

The third choice, **Control AutoCorrect Options** let us edit the default formatting for Text Boxes.

Memo to Self: You may or may not have this option, depending on your settings. Keep going: let's find out what AutoFit can do.

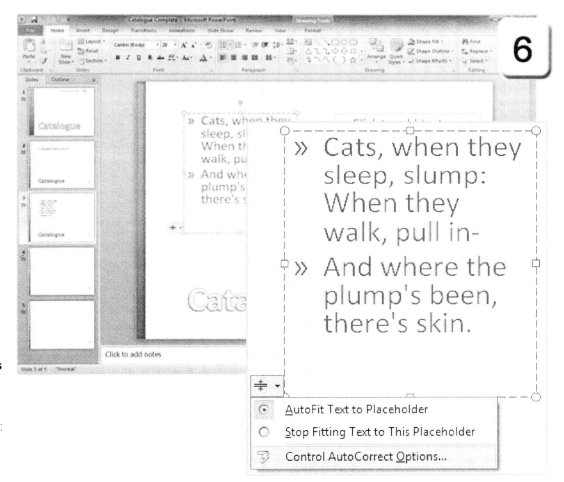

Exam 77-883: Microsoft PowerPoint 2010
2. Creating a Slide Presentation
2.6. Format text boxes: Use AutoFit

Text Box AutoFit Options

You can see the AutoCorrect option by clicking the little pop up, or by right clicking the Text Box and going to Format Shape. Either way, you will see there are four tabs in the **Control AutoCorrect Options**. The AutoFit options can be found on the one called **AutoFormat As You Type**.

7. Try it: Review the AutoFormat
Microsoft Office has many **AutoFormat** settings that you can turn on or off. By default, PowerPoint will replace fractions, hyphens, hyperlinks and even emoticons (smiley faces.)

There are more options. Click CANCEL and keep going, please.

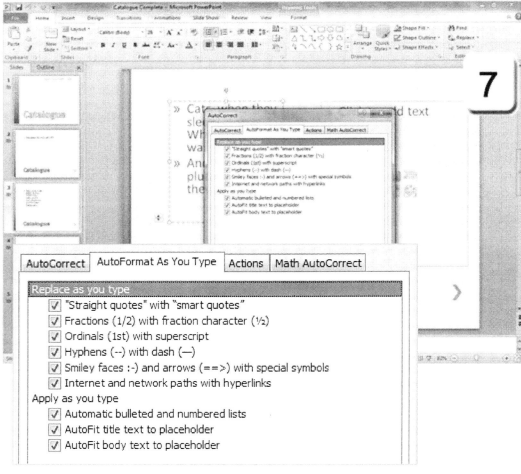

Exam 77-883: Microsoft PowerPoint 2010
2. Creating a Slide Presentation
2.6. Format text boxes: Use AutoFit

Format with Drawing Tools

When you select a Text Box you should see the **Drawing Tools**. We looked at an abbreviated set of Drawing Tools on the Home Ribbon. Let's look at the options on the Drawing Tools Ribbon.

8. Try it: Review the Drawing Tools
The Text Box on Slide 3 is selected. The Drawing Tools should be available.
Go to the **Format** Ribbon.

What Do You See? The Shape Styles include the same options that were available on the Home and Design Ribbons: Shape Fill, Outline and Effects.

Look in the bottom right corner of the **Shape Styles** group for the option arrow. Click that arrow and keep going...!

Drawing Tools ->Format

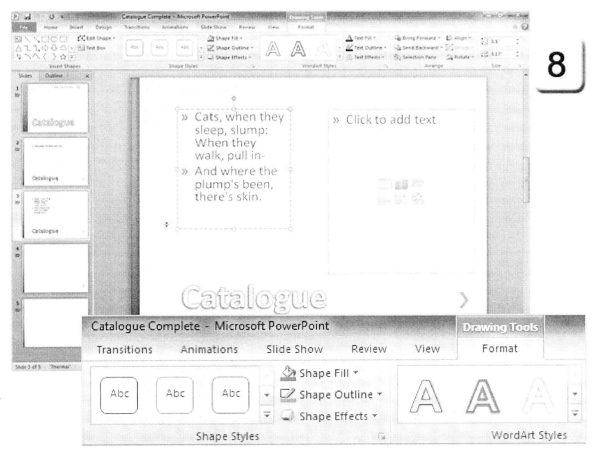

Exam 77-883: Microsoft PowerPoint 2010
2. Creating a Slide Presentation
2.6. Format text boxes: Use the Drawing Tools

Text Box Formatting

There are about a dozen categories that you can edit when you Format the Shape. You will find **Text Box** at the bottom of the list on the left side of this dialogue box.

9. Try it: Format the Text Box
Text Layout includes the following:
Vertical alignment (Top, Middle, Bottom)
Text direction (Horizontal, Rotate, Stacked)

AutoFit has three choices:
Do not Autofit.
Shrink text on overflow.
Resize shape to fit text.

You can also edit the **Internal margins**: Left, Right, Top and Bottom. By default PowerPoint will **Wrap text in shape**.

Very good. Click **Close** to return to the slides.

Drawing Tools ->Format-> Shape Styles->More

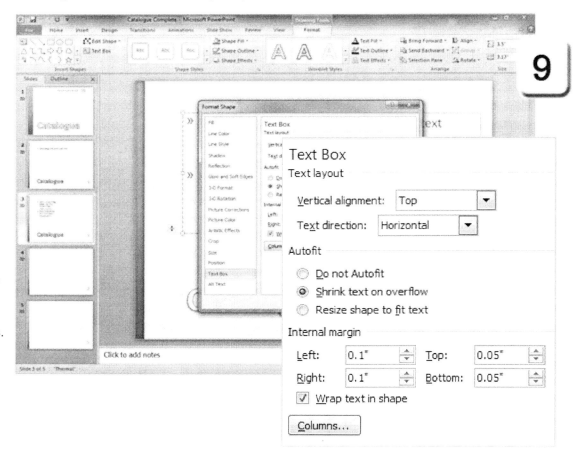

Exam 77-883: Microsoft PowerPoint 2010
2. Creating a Slide Presentation
2.6. Format text boxes: Wrap text in shape

Format the Text Box Size

A few minutes ago you resized the Text Box by dragging one of the Shape handles. Here is a more precise method to format the **Size**.

1. Try it: Format the Size of a Text Box
Go to Slide 3 and select the Text Box.
Go to **Drawing Tools->Format->Size**.
Type the **Width**: 3.25"

2. What Do You See? When you changed the width, the height may not always resize proportionately. In the example on this page the height stayed the same.

Our lessons have looked at Text, Text Boxes, Pictures and Shapes. Each of these objects can be customized with the **Drawing Tools**. OK, that's enough about **Shapes** for a minute.

Drawing Tools ->Format-> Size

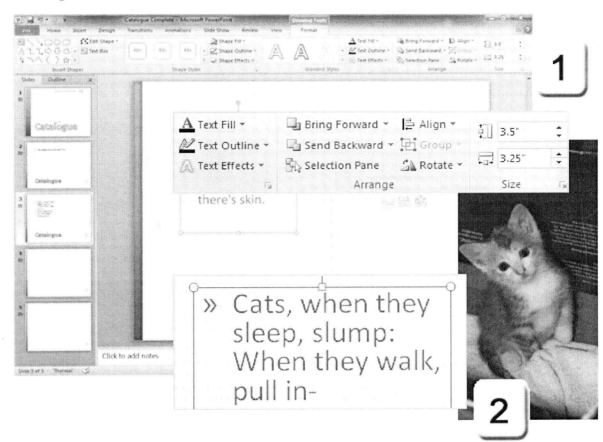

Exam 77-883: Microsoft PowerPoint 2010
2. Creating a Slide Presentation
2.6. Format text boxes: Format the Size

SmartArt Graphics

Some Shapes are very dynamic...in fact, they are called **SmartArt**. The Shapes in a SmartArt diagram automatically update based on your text.

1. Try it: Insert SmartArt
Select Slide 4.
Go to **Insert ->Illustrations->SmartArt.**
Choose a SmartArt Graphic
The SmartArt library includes:
List
Process
Cycle
Hierarchy
Relationship
Matrix
Pyramid
Office.com

Select: **Hierarchy** and keep going, please.

What Do You See? As you click on each option, you should see a sample of the chart, as well as, a short description of the purpose of this diagram.

Insert ->Illustrations->SmartArt

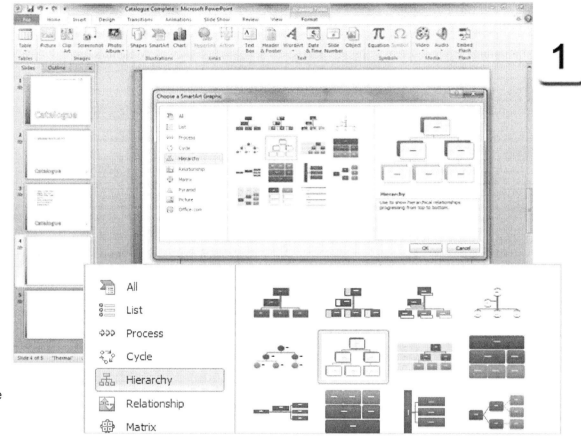

Exam 77-883: Microsoft PowerPoint 2010
3. Working with Graphical and Multimedia Elements
3.4. Manipulate SmartArt

Hello, SmartArt

You should see a new SmartArt diagram in your slide.

2. Try it: Review the SmartArt Tools
There are two **SmartArt Tools**: Design and Format. The **Design** Ribbon has options for creating and editing the SmartArt graphic. The **Format** Ribbon includes options that are similar to the Drawing Tools.

Keep going...

SmartArt Tools

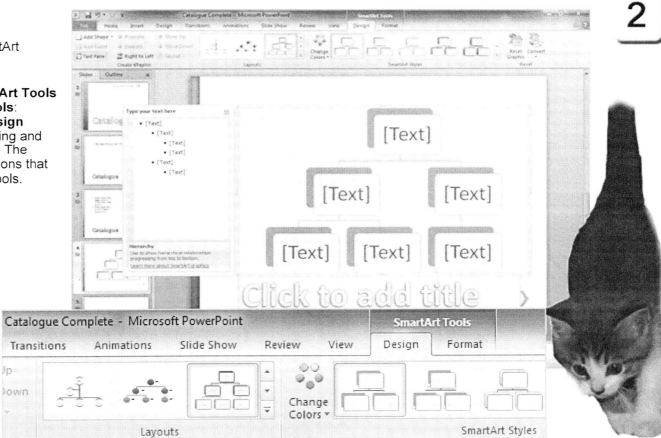

Exam 77-883: Microsoft PowerPoint 2010
3. Working with Graphical and Multimedia Elements
3.4. Manipulate SmartArt

View the Text Pane

The SmartArt has two parts: the Graphic and the **Text Pane**. The Text Pane is the outline to the left of the SmartArt diagram. You can Show or Hide the Text Pane if you wish.

3. Try This: View the Text Pane
Click on the SmartArt diagram.
Go to **SmartArt Tools ->Design**.
Go to **Create Graphic**.
Select: **Text Pane**.

What Do You See? The **Text Pane** can be displayed or hidden.

What Else Do You See? When you close the Text Box look on the left side of the SmartArt Diagram for a small set of arrows that you can use to Show the Text Pane again.

Keep going...

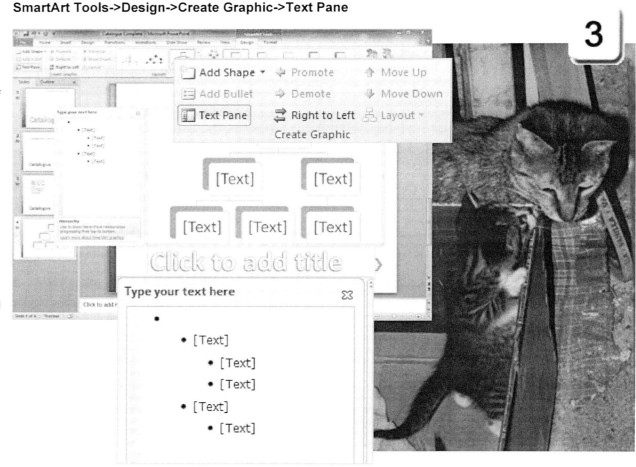

Exam 77-883: Microsoft PowerPoint 2010
3. Working with Graphical and Multimedia Elements
3.4. Manipulate SmartArt: View the Text Pane

Edit the SmartArt Text

4. Try it: Type your text here

Type the following:

- Catalogue
    - Dogs
        - Pluto
        - Goofy
    - Cats

What Do You See? Whatever you type in the Text Box will be displayed in the Diagram. Keep going...

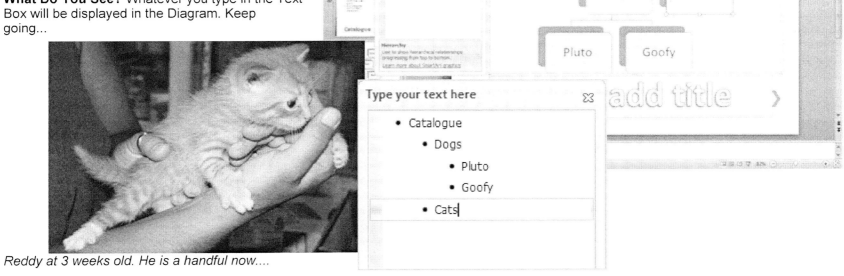

Reddy at 3 weeks old. He is a handful now....

Exam 77-883: Microsoft PowerPoint 2010
3. Working with Graphical and Multimedia Elements
3.4. Manipulate SmartArt

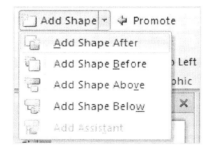

Add Shapes

5. Try it: Add More Shapes
The SmartArt is selected on Slide 4.
Click after "Cats" in the Text Box.
Go to **SmartArt Tools->Design.**
Go to **Create Graphic.**
Click on **Add Shape.**
Select: **Add Shape After.**
Type: Mice

What Do You See? When you add a Shape before or after SmartArt places the new Shape in the same bullet level as the Shape you selected.

Keep going...

SmartArt Tools->Design->Create Graphic->Add Shape

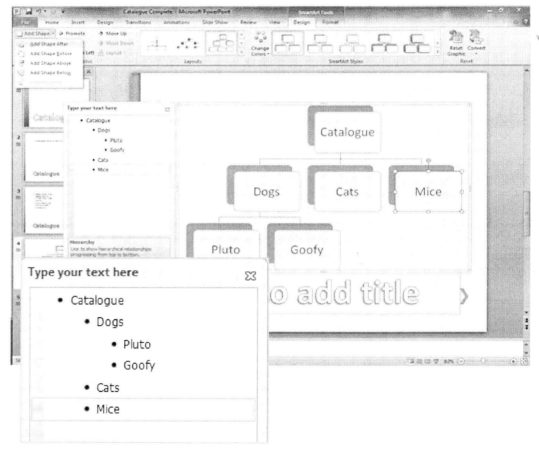

Exam 77-883: Microsoft PowerPoint 2010
3. Working with Graphical and Multimedia Elements
3.4. Manipulate SmartArt: Add and Remove Shapes

Manipulate SmartArt

Promote and **Demote** are used to change the bullet level of a Shape.

Before You Begin: Add More Shapes
The SmartArt is selected on Slide 4.
Click after "Mice" in the Text Box.
Go to **SmartArt Tools->Design**.
Go to **Create Graphic**.
Click on **Add Shape**.
Select: **Add Shape Below**.
Type: Mickey

Keep going...

At 4 weeks old the kittens are ready to play....

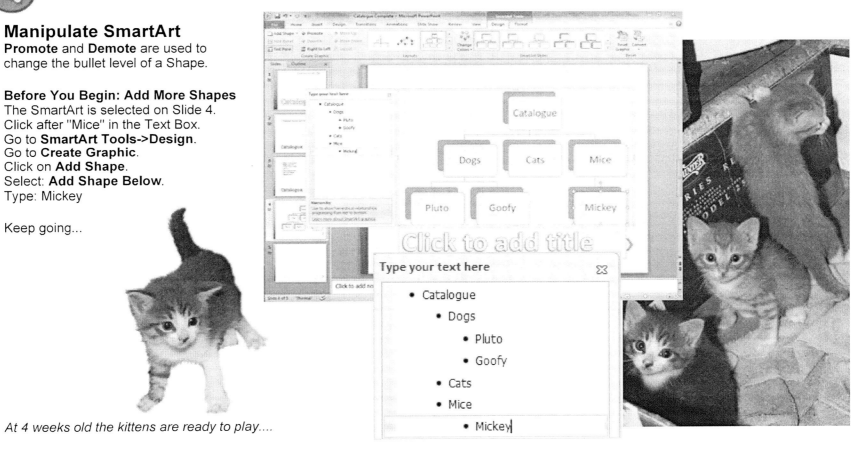

Exam 77-883: Microsoft PowerPoint 2010
3. Working with Graphical and Multimedia Elements
3.4. Manipulate SmartArt: Add and Remove Shapes

Promote or Demote a Shape

6. Try it: Promote a Shape
The SmartArt is selected on Slide 4.
Click after "Mickey" in the Text Box.
Go to **SmartArt Tools->Design.**
Go to **Create Graphic->Promote.**

What Do You See? The "Mickey" Shape was moved to the bullet level above the one it was on.

Try This, Too: Demote a Shape
Click after "Mickey" in the Text Box.
Go to **SmartArt Tools->Design.**
Go to **Create Graphic->Promote.**

The "Mickey" Shape should be back in the bullet level below the one it was on when you selected it. OK, that makes sense.

Keep going...

SmartArt Tools->Design->Create Graphic->Promote

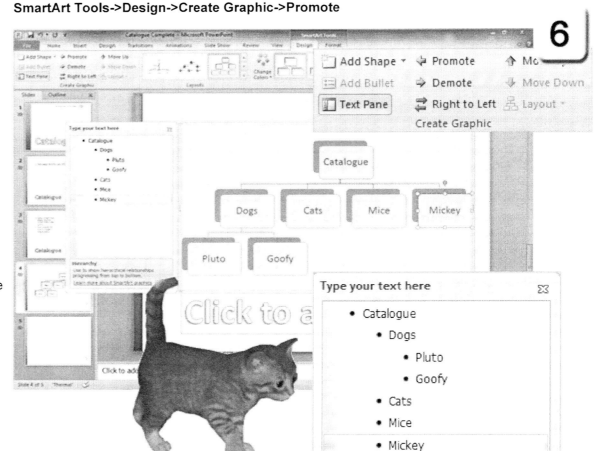

Exam 77-883: Microsoft PowerPoint 2010
3. Working with Graphical and Multimedia Elements
3.4. Manipulate SmartArt: Promote or Demote

Reorder the Shapes

Say you wanted to change this graphic so that the order is reversed and the Shapes go Right-to-Left. Here are the steps.

7. Try it: Reorder the Shapes
The SmartArt is selected on Slide 4.
Go to **SmartArt Tools->Design**.
Go to **Create Graphic->Right to Left.**

What Do You See? The Shapes were reordered so that they are the opposite of the original layout: Dog, Cats, Mice. Keep going...!

Memo to Self: In the world of cartoons, everybody knows the hierarchy goes: Mice, then Cats, then Dogs, right?

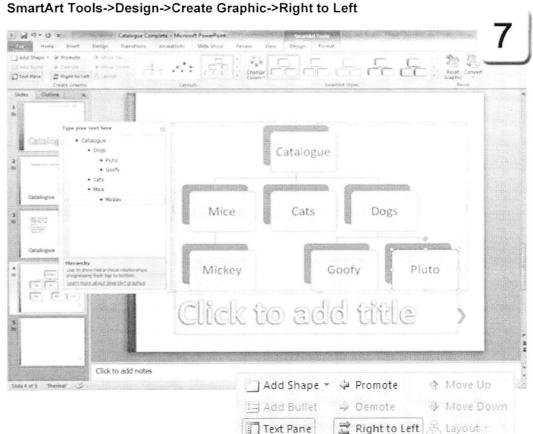

Exam 77-883: Microsoft PowerPoint 2010
3. Working with Graphical and Multimedia Elements
3.4. Manipulate SmartArt: Reorder the Shapes

Edit the Layout

There are many **Layout** templates that you can choose. Some are vertical (organizing the Shapes from top to bottom) and some are horizontal (arranging the Shapes from left to right.) Let's look at the options.

8. Try it: Edit the Layout
The SmartArt is selected on Slide 4.
Go to **SmartArt Tools->Design**.
Go to **Layout**.
Select: **Horizontal Organization Chart**.

What Do You See? The Shapes on the page are in a horizontal **Layout**.

What Else Do You See? The hierarchy was changed so that the Dogs are back on top. You can go to **Move Up** if you wish to put the Mice back on top.

Keep going, please.

SmartArt Tools->Design-> Layout

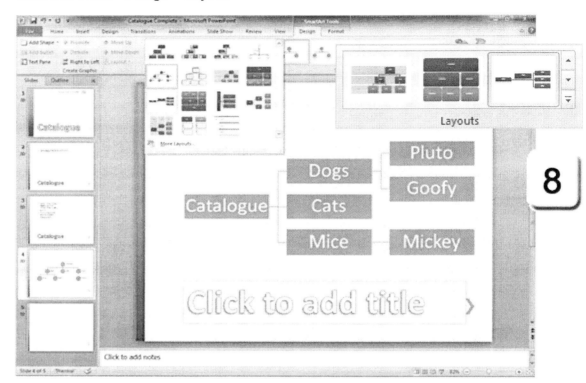

Exam 77-883: Microsoft PowerPoint 2010
3. Working with Graphical and Multimedia Elements
3.4. Manipulate SmartArt: Edit the Layout

Styles: Change the Color

We have talked about color often in these pages. Colors can invoke trust, joy, good will and faithfulness, purity and darkness. The **SmartArt Styles** include **Color** as well as **Styles**. Let's start with the Color.

9. Try it: Change the Color
The SmartArt is selected on Slide 4.
Go to **SmartArt Tools->Design.**
Go to **SmartArt Styles-> Change Color.**
Select: **Colorful Range.**

What Do You See? The Colors are applied Left to Right, not Top to Bottom in this Layout. Keep going...

Cats sleep fat!

9

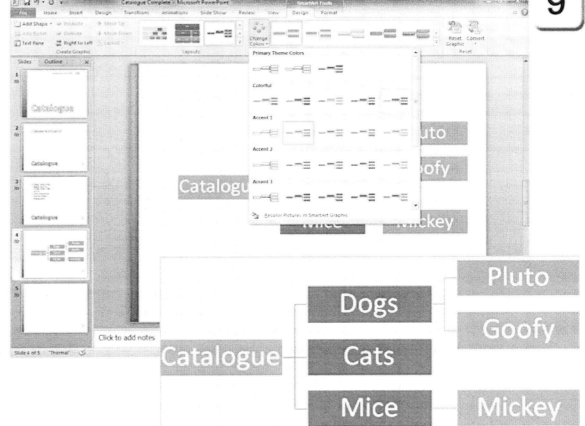

Exam 77-883: Microsoft PowerPoint 2010
3. Working with Graphical and Multimedia Elements
3.4. Manipulate SmartArt: Change the Color

More SmartArt Styles

Last, but not least, you can change the **SmartArt Style**.

Try it: Choose a SmartArt Style
The SmartArt is selected on Slide 4.
Go to **SmartArt Tools->Design.**
Go to **SmartArt Styles-> Styles.**
Select: **Intense Effect.**

What Do You See? SmartArt, like all of the Shapes, can be formatted with Styles. The Computer Mama likes the Styles because they format so many aspects of the Shape including color, shadows, glow and bevel.

So far, so good for the **Design** Ribbon.

Fat cat!

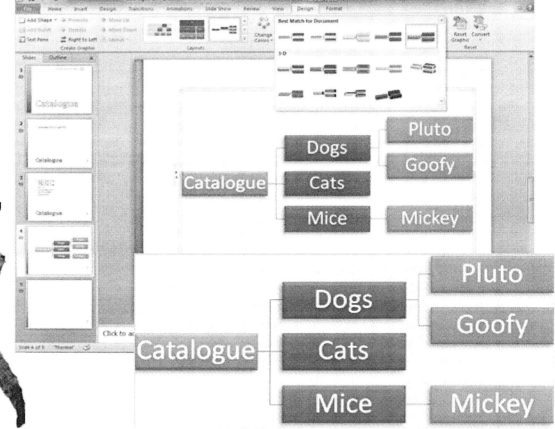

Exam 77-883: Microsoft PowerPoint 2010
3. Working with Graphical and Multimedia Elements
3.4. Manipulate SmartArt: Choose a Style

Format the SmartArt

This discussion has focused on the SmartArt **Design** Ribbon. Let's review the options on the second Ribbon in the SmartArt Tools: **Format.**

1. Try it: Review the Format Ribbon
The SmartArt is selected on Slide 4.
One of the Shapes is selected.
Go to **SmartArt Tools->Format.**

What Do You See? The SmartArt **Format** Ribbon has many of the same options as the Drawing Tools:
Shapes
Shape Styles
WordArt Styles
Arrange
Size

Keep going...

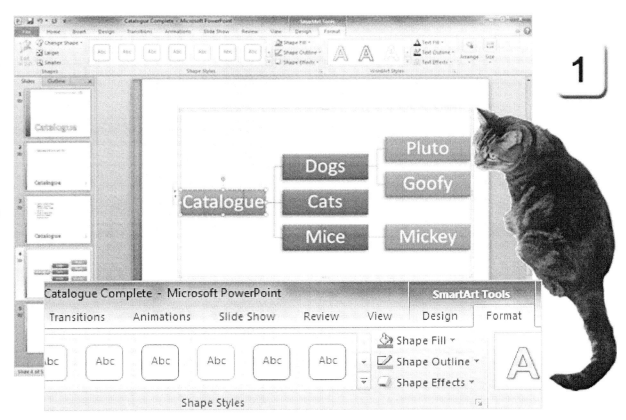

Exam 77-883: Microsoft PowerPoint 2010
3. Working with Graphical and Multimedia Elements
3.4. Manipulate SmartArt: Format

Format: Change the Shape

You can **Change the Shape** in the Smart Art if you wish. In this example we will select one Shape and format it differently than the rest in this graphic.

2. Try it: Change the Shape
The SmartArt is selected on Slide 4.
Select the "Catalogue" Shape.
Go to **SmartArt Tools->Format.**
Click on **Change Shape.**
Select: **Oval.**

What Do You See? You can choose any of the Shapes: Rectangles, Basic, Block, Equation, Flowchart. Stars and Banners, Callouts and Action Buttons.

What Else Do You See? The SmartArt formatting was applied to the new Shape.

Keep going...

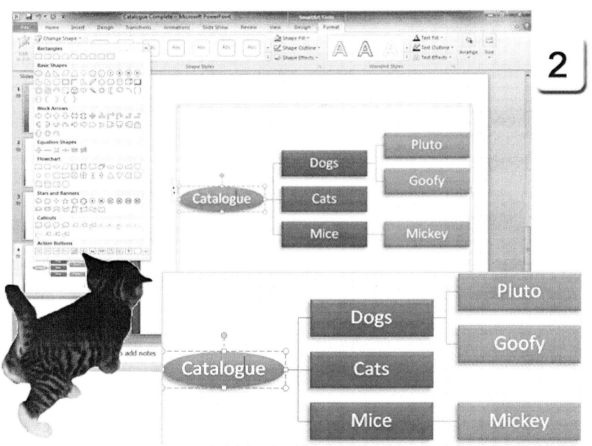

Exam 77-883: Microsoft PowerPoint 2010
3. Working with Graphical and Multimedia Elements
3.4. Manipulate SmartArt: Change the Shape

Format Shapes: Larger

Shapes can also have different sizes.

3. Try it: Make the Shape Larger
The SmartArt is selected on Slide 4.
The "Catalogue" Shape is selected.
Go to **SmartArt Tools->Format-> Shapes.**
Click on **Larger.**

What Do You See? Each time you click on **Larger**, the Shape increases in size. As the Shape gets larger, the other Shapes become smaller to fit the SmartArt graphic.

Of course, there is more...

You can't be too thin or too rich...

SmartArt Tools->Format->Shapes->Larger

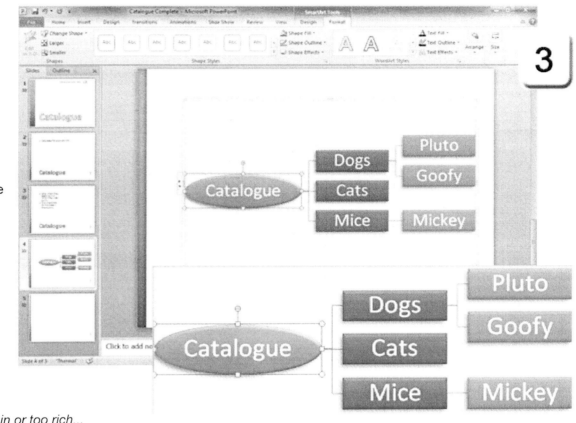

Exam 77-883: Microsoft PowerPoint 2010
3. Working with Graphical and Multimedia Elements
3.4. Manipulate SmartArt: Change the Shape Size

Format the SmartArt Size

Earlier, we changed the Size of one Shape. You can edit the **Size** of the SmartArt graphic as well.

Before You Begin: Select the SmartArt graphic on Slide 4. Copy and Paste the SmartArt to Slide 5.

4. Try it: Change the SmartArt Size
The SmartArt is selected on Slide 5.
Go to **SmartArt Tools->Format->Size.**
Change the Width: **4"**
Click ENTER on the keyboard.

What Do You See? The SmartArt was **Resized** proportionally: height and width.

Keep going...

SmartArt Tools->Format->Size

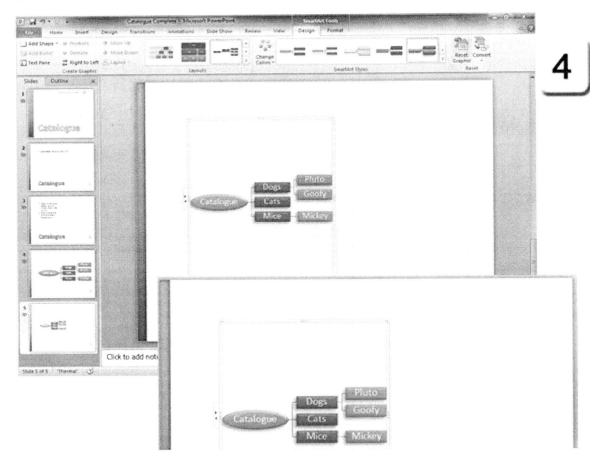

Exam 77-883: Microsoft PowerPoint 2010
3. Working with Graphical and Multimedia Elements
3.4. Manipulate SmartArt

Convert the SmartArt: Text

The SmartArt Design Ribbon has a couple of interesting tools for **Converting** the SmartArt into Text or Graphics.

Before You Begin: There are two ways you can Convert the SmartArt. Please copy and paste the small SmartArt graphic on Slide 5 so we can try both options.

5. Try it: Convert the SmartArt to Text
The first SmartArt is selected on Slide 5.
Go to **SmartArt Tools->Design.**
Go to **Reset->Convert.**
Click on **Convert to Text.**

What Do You See? The SmartArt has been **Converted** to a bulleted list.

Keep going...

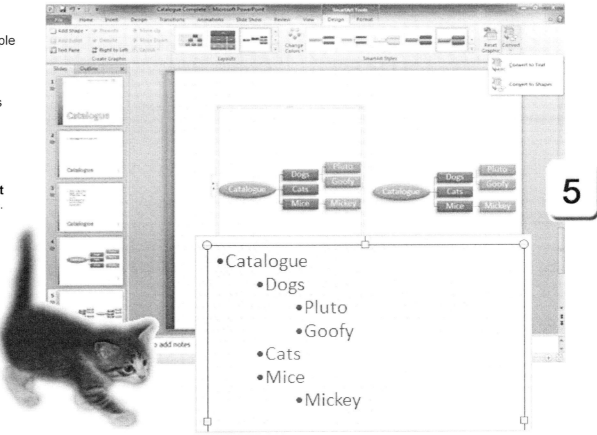

Exam 77-883: Microsoft PowerPoint 2010
3. Working with Graphical and Multimedia Elements
3.4. Manipulate SmartArt: Convert to Text

SmartArt Tools->Design->Reset->Convert->Convert to Shapes

Convert the SmartArt: Shapes

6. Try it: Convert the SmartArt to Text
The second SmartArt is selected on Slide 5.
Go to **SmartArt Tools->Design.**
Go to **Reset->Convert.**
Click on **Convert to Shapes.**

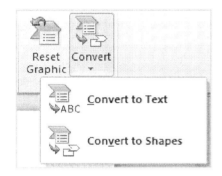

What Do You See? The SmartArt has been Converted to Shapes. The **Drawing Tools** are now available.

So, we are back to where we started.
Allez, allez in free.

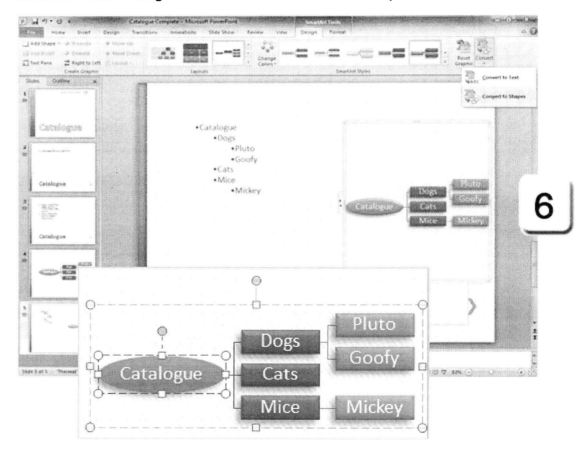

Exam 77-883: Microsoft PowerPoint 2010
3. Working with Graphical and Multimedia Elements
3.4. Manipulate SmartArt: Convert to Shapes

Summary

Try This: Save Your Presentation
Go to **File->Save.**
Browse to your Documents folder.
Name the File: Catalogue.pptx. Click **Save**.

Summary
This lesson introduced Shapes and SmartArt. The Shapes and SmartArt offer another way to visualize a concept. SmartArt is a fun, dynamic and easy to update. The SmartArt Tools are similar to the options that you would find on the Drawing Tools Ribbon for a Shape.

Well, you done good. You get two cookies.

Curious as a kitten!

Practice Activities

Lesson 6: Shapes and SmartArt

Try This: Do the following steps

1. Open a new, blank presentation.
2. On the Title Slide, add the Title: Preschool Primer
   a. Resize the font to size 88. Change the alignment to Bottom. Align the text Right.
3. Add a new slide. Insert SmartArt Cycle: Basic Cycle. Add the following seasons using the Text Pane: Spring, Winter, Fall, Summer.
   a. Add the Label Big. Add the following in the Big List: Elephant, Horse, Lion,
   b. Add the Label Small. Add the following in the Small List: cat, mouse, raccoon
   c. Remove any extra shapes
   d. Change the SmartArt Style to Cartoon.
   e. Change the Shape Art Color to Colorful Range—Accent Colors 4 to 5
   f. Change the Smart Art layout to Hierarchy List

5. Add a new slide. Insert Smart Art Cycle Matrix.
   a. Add the following text to the wedges in the circle: Pets, Farm, Forest, Bugs
   b. For Pets: add Cat to List Level 2, add dog to List Level 2
   c. For Farm: Add Cow to List Level 2, add Horse to List Level 2
   d. For Forest: Add Bear to List Level 2, add Deer to List Level 2
   e. For Bugs: Add Spider to List Level 2, add Ladybug to List Level 2
   f. Change the Smart Art color to Colored Outline, accent 2
   g. Convert the SmartArt to Shapes
   h. Delete the arrow shapes in the center of the Cycle Matrix

6. Add a new slide. Add the following numbered list:
   1. Sun
   2. Shoes
   3. Tree
   4. Doors
   5. Hives
   6. Sticks
   7. Heaven
   8. Gate
   9. Line
   10. Hen

   a. Change the Text Direction to Stacked.

   b. Resize the text box, if necessary, so Heaven and Sticks fit

7. Save the file as Beginning PowerPoint Practice Activity 5

Guard Cat watches the printer...keep going

Test Yourself

1. Which Ribbon is available when you select a Text Box?
a. Drawing Tools
b. Text Box Tools
c. Shape Tools
Tip: Beginning PowerPoint, page 167

2. To access the Drawing Tools Ribbon, select a Text Box.
a. True
b. False
Tip: Beginning PowerPoint, page 167

3. Which are Autofit options for a text box? (Give all correct answers)
a. Do not Autofit
b. Shrink Text on overflow
c. Resize shape to fit text

Tip: Beginning PowerPoint, page 168

4. Which are types of Smart Art? (Give all correct answers)
a. List
b. Process
c. Cycle
d. Matrix
e. Procedures
Tip: Beginning PowerPoint, page 170

5. Which are Smart Art Tools Ribbons? (Give all correct answers)
a. Design
b. Format
c. Styles
Tip: Beginning PowerPoint, page 171

6. You can change the color of Smart Art.
a. True
b. False
Tip: Beginning PowerPoint, page 179

7. Styles can be applied to Smart Art.
a. True
b. False
Tip: Beginning PowerPoint, page 180

8. Which of the following are found on the Smart Art Tools Format Ribbon? (Give all correct answers)
a. Shapes
b. Shape Styles
c. Word Art Styles
d. Arrange
e. Size
Tip: Beginning PowerPoint, page 181

9. Smart Art cannot be converted to text.
a. True
b. False
Tip: Beginning PowerPoint, page 185

10. Smart Art can be converted to individual shapes
a. True
b. False
Tip: Beginning PowerPoint, page 186

She thinks it's her job to change the ink...keep going

Catalogue

Cats sleep fat and walk thin.

Cats, when they sleep, slump; When they walk, pull in--
And where the plump's been, there's skin.

Cats walk thin.

Cats wait in a lump. Jump in a streak.
Cats, when they jump, are sleek
As a grape slipping its skin--They have technique.
Oh, cats don't creak. They sneak.

Cats sleep fat.

They spread comfort beneath them Like a good mat,
As if they picked the place And then sat.
You walk around one As if he were the City Hall after that.

If male, A cat is apt to sing upon a major scale:
This concert is for everybody, this Is wholesale.

For a baton, he wields a tail.
(He is also found, When happy, to resound
With an enclosed and private sound.)
A cat condenses.

He pulls in his tail to go under bridges,
And himself to go under fences. Cats fit in any size box or kit;
And if a large pumpkin grew under one, He could arch over it.

When everyone else is just ready to go out,
The cat is just ready to come in.
He's not where he's been.

Cats sleep fat and walk thin.

--Rosalie Moore (B. 1910)

Well done, O faithful servant.

PowerPoint 2010: Working with Graphics

Here's Looking at You, Kid

Beginning PowerPoint Objectives
In this lesson, you will learn how to:

1. Use the **Home** Ribbon to create a **Photo Album**

2. Add images to the Photo Album in black and white

3. Adjust the Photo Album images: Brightness and Contrast, Rotation and Size

4. Use the **Home** Ribbon to add slides from other PowerPoint presentations and format the **Sections**

5. Use the **View** Ribbon to work with multiple shows

© 2011 Comma Productions LLC

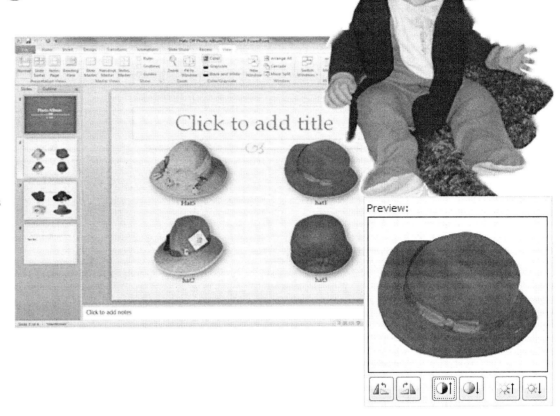

Lesson 7: Photo Albums and Views

1. Readings

Read Lesson 7 in the Beginning PowerPoint guide, page 191-243.

Project

A presentation that combines several slide shows into one and formats the sections.

Downloads

Spring Has Sprung.pptx
Spring Forward, Fall Back.pptx
Song of Solomon.pptx
hat1.gif, hat2.gif, hat3.gif, hat4.gif
hat5.gif, hat6.gif, hat7.gif, hat8.gif
Hat-and-Hatbox.gif
Sandhill Cranes.pptx
Extra for Experts.pptx

2. Practice

Do the Practice Activity on page 244.

3. Assessment

Review the Test questions on page 245

View Ribbon

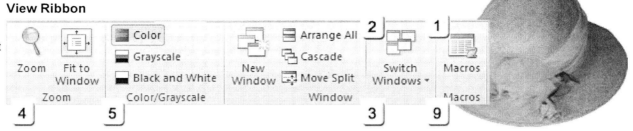

Home Ribbon

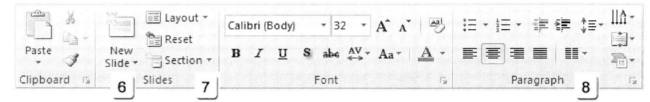

Menu Maps

From the **View Ribbon**.
1. View ->Switch Windows, page 205
2. View ->Window->Arrange All, page 206
3. View ->Window->Cascade, page 207
4. View ->Window->Zoom, page 208
5. View ->Color/Grayscale, page 209

Not pictured above:
9. View->Presentation Views, page 220

More Menu Maps

From the **Home Ribbon**
6. Home ->Slides->New Slide->Reuse Slides, page 211
7. Home->Slides->Section->Add Section, page 215
8. Home->Paragraph->Columns, page 242

Slide Shows and Views

So far we have been working with the elements of a slide show: Text, Text Boxes, Pictures, Shapes and SmartArt. This lesson shows you how to put it all together. We will begin by creating a simple **Photo Album**. Then, we will add slides from some of the presentations we created earlier. There will be several presentations open at the same time, so we will also look at the different **Views** you can use in PowerPoint.

Start -> All Programs ->Microsoft Office-> Microsoft Office PowerPoint 2010

Please Start Microsoft PowerPoint
What do you see at the top of the screen? Is there a Title Bar that says Microsoft PowerPoint? Yes.

Is there a **Home** Ribbon with the Clipboard, Font and Paragraph Groups? Yes.

If your screen looks similar to the example on this page, then you are ready to get started.

Before You Begin

This lesson begins with a Photo Album. Before you begin, please download the sample pictures. You will also need to download the sample presentations if you did not save the slide shows that we created in the beginning lessons.

1. Try it: Create a New Presentation
Open Microsoft PowerPoint 2010. You should see a new, blank presentation.
Select the Title Text Box on Slide 1.
Type: Hat's Off to Spring!
Insert a Picture: Hat-and-Hat-Box.

Do This: Save the Presentation
Go to **File->Save.**
Browse to your Document folder.
File Name: Hats Off to Spring
Click: **SAVE.**
Keep going...

Memo to Self: You do not have to MATCH the images and special effects shown on these pages. Please add your own pictures if you wish.

Microsoft PowerPoint

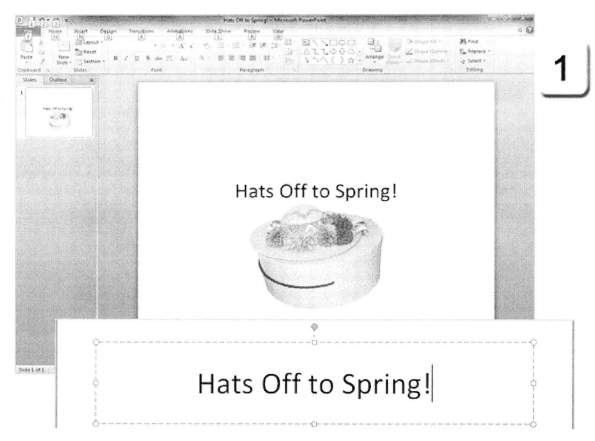

Exam 77-883: Microsoft PowerPoint 2010
2. Creating a Slide Presentation
2.5. Enter and format text

Insert a Photo Album

2. Try it: Insert a Photo Album
Go to **Insert ->Images->Photo Album**.
Click on **New Photo Album**.

Keep going...

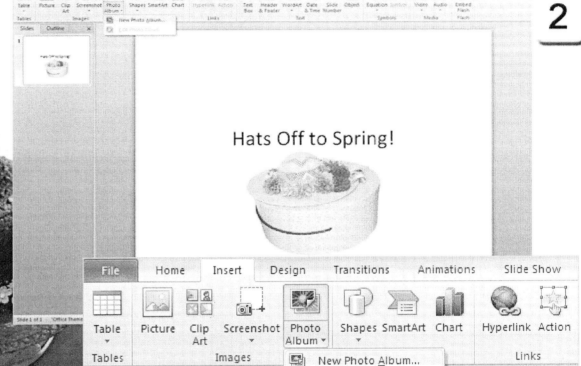

2

Exam 77-883: Microsoft PowerPoint 2010
2. Creating a Slide Presentation
2.1. Construct and edit photo albums

Photo Album Options

3. Try it: Review the Photo Album Options
There are four options that you can edit when you create a new Photo Album. They include:

Album Content
Insert pictures and Insert Text

Picture Options
Captions below All pictures
All pictures black and white

Album Layout
Picture layout
Frame shape
Theme

What Do You See? Most of the options are grayed out. They will be available when you add some pictures.

Keep going...

Insert ->Images->Photo Album

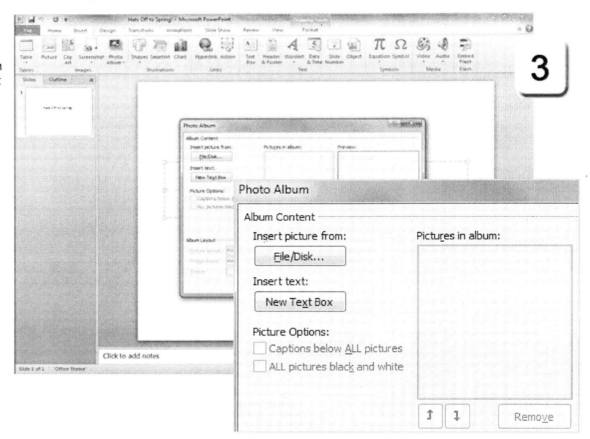

Exam 77-883: Microsoft PowerPoint 2010
2. Creating a Slide Presentation
2.1. Construct and edit photo albums

Photo Album Content

4. Try it: Insert Picture from File
Click on **File/Disk**.
Browse to the folder with your pictures.
Select the 8 sample hat pictures.

What Do You See? The names of the pictures are listed in **Pictures in album**. When you select a picture you can see a **Preview** on the right.

So far, so good. Keep going, please.

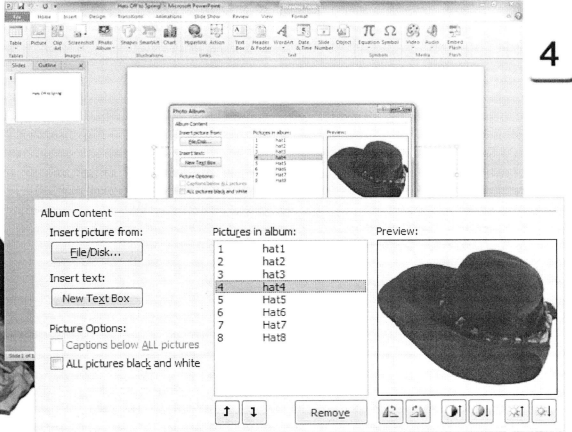

Exam 77-883: Microsoft PowerPoint 2010
2. Creating a Slide Presentation
2.1. Construct and edit photo albums

Adjust the Pictures

In any bunch of pictures there will be a wide range of exposures. Some of them may be light and others may be dark. You can adjust each picture in the album if need be.

There are three adjustments under the Preview:
Rotation (rotate left and right)
Contrast (increase and decrease)
Brightness (increase and decrease)

5. Try it: Adjust the Picture
Go to Pictures in album.
Select hat1.

Change the Rotation: Right
Change the Contrast: Increase
Change the Brightness: Increase

What So You See? When you increase the Contrast and Brightness you should see that hat1 has a hatband that was hidden in the darkness.

Keep going...

Insert ->Images->Photo Album

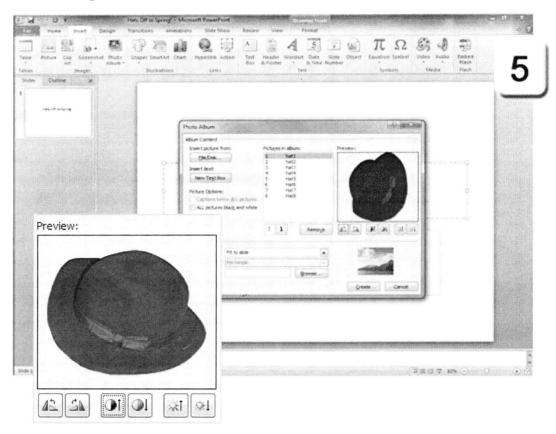

Exam 77-883: Microsoft PowerPoint 2010
2. Creating a Slide Presentation
2.1. Construct and edit photo albums: Adjust the Rotation, Contrast and Brightness

Reorder the Pictures

You probably already guessed that you can use the arrows to the left of the Remove button.

6. Try it: Reorder the Pictures
Go to the Pictures in album.
Select Hat5.
Use the Up arrow to move Hat5 to the top of the list.

Keep going...

Insert ->Images->Photo Album

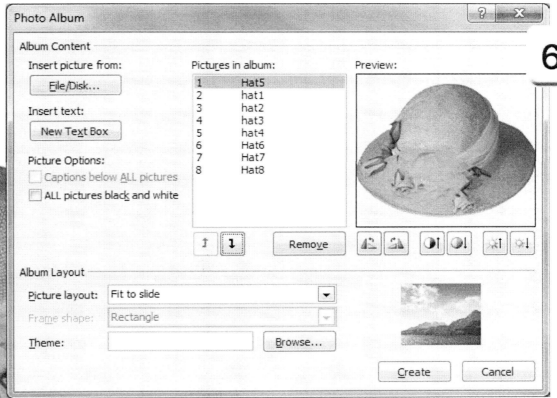

Exam 77-883: Microsoft PowerPoint 2010
2. Creating a Slide Presentation
2.1. Construct and edit photo albums: Reorder the Pictures

Edit the Album Layout

There are two types of **Picture layouts**: with and without Title. The Picture layouts come with 1, 2 and 4 pictures per slide.

7. Try it: Edit the Album Layout
Go to the Album Layout.
Choose a Picture Layout: 4 pictures with title

What Do You See? You can also select a different **Frame shape** if you wish. The default Frame shape is a Rectangle, but the list includes Rounded Rectangle, Simple Frame (black or white), Compound Frame and two options with Shadows.

What Else Do You See? There are two **Picture Options** available, now:
Captions below ALL pictures
All pictures black and white.

Select: **Captions below ALL pictures**

Memo to Self: The option to add **Captions** isn't available until you choose a Layout that includes Text.

Insert ->Images->Photo Album

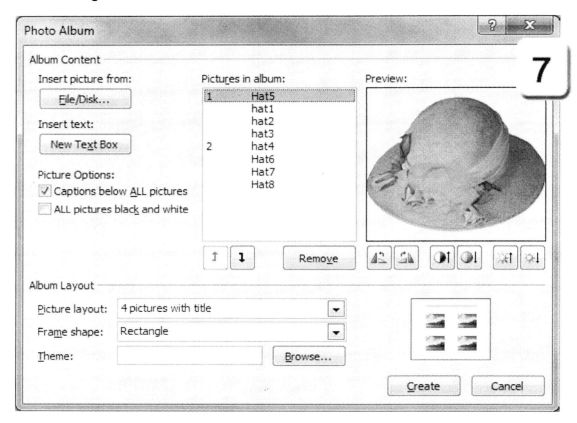

Exam 77-883: Microsoft PowerPoint 2010
2. Creating a Slide Presentation
2.1. Construct and edit photo albums: Edit the Album Layout

Create the Photo Album

8. Try it: Create the Photo Album
When you click **Create**, PowerPoint will make a NEW presentation.

What Do You See? Each picture is nestled in a **Shape** that has a Text Box for the Caption. You can edit the Caption if you wish.

What Else Do You See? When you select a Shape you should see the **Drawing** and **Picture Tools**.

Keep going...

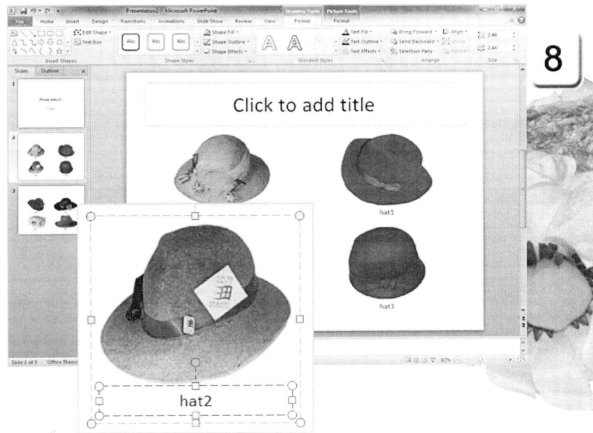

Exam 77-883: Microsoft PowerPoint 2010
2. Creating a Slide Presentation
2.1. Construct and edit photo albums: Edit the Captions

Edit the Photo Album

Say you wanted to edit the Photo Album and add a Text Box. Here are the steps.

9. Try it: Sample
Go to **Insert ->Images->Photo Album**.
Click on **Edit Photo Album**.

Go to **Album Content->Insert Text**.
Click on New Text Box.

What Do You See? A new Text Box will be placed on Slide 3 in this Photo Album.

OK, click **UPDATE** to save your changes.

Insert ->Images->Photo Album->Edit Photo Album

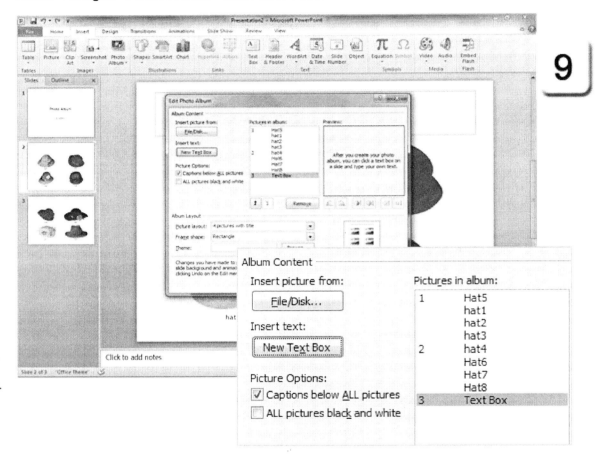

Exam 77-883: Microsoft PowerPoint 2010
2. Creating a Slide Presentation
2.1. Construct and edit photo albums: Add a Text Box

OK, Dress it Up
1. Try it: Add a Theme
Go to **Design ->Theme**
Select a **Theme**: Hard Cover

2. Try This, Too: Add an Effect
Select each photo.
Go to **Picture Tools->Format.**
Go to **Picture Styles.**
Select a **Style**: Drop Shadow.

The Drop Shadow gives the images
depth: they look *real* not flat.

Do This: Save the Photo Album
Go to **File->Save.**
Browse to your Document folder.
File Name: Hats Off Photo Album.
Click: **SAVE.**

Design ->Theme

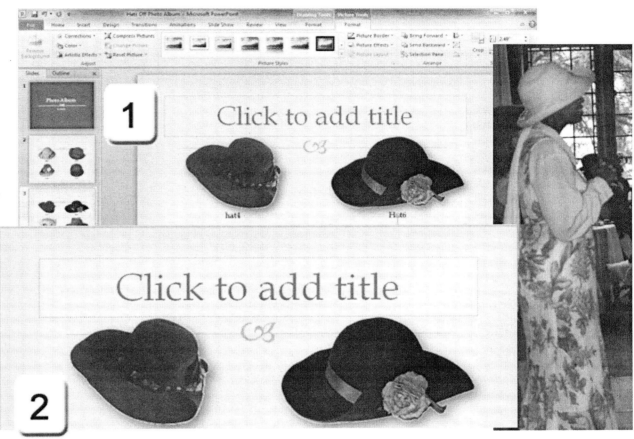

Exam 77-883: Microsoft PowerPoint 2010
2. Creating a Slide Presentation
2.4. Format slides: Apply a Theme

Working with Two Shows

The Photo Album is a different slide show than the one we began with: Hats Off to Spring. The Photo Album is on top of the Hats Off presentation. One Window is hiding the other. Let's look at the option for working with multiple presentations.

1. Try it: Review the View Ribbon

Go to the **View** Ribbon. The groups are:
Presentation Views
Master Views
Show
Zoom
Color/Grayscale
Window
Macros

View Ribbon

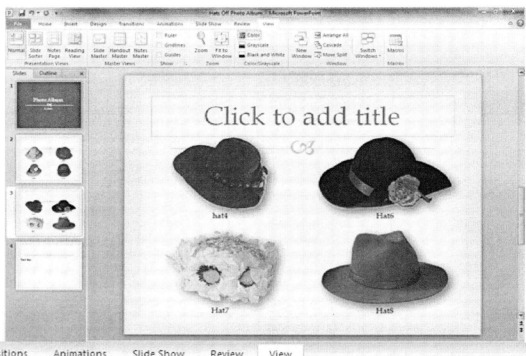

Exam 77-883: Microsoft PowerPoint 2010
1. Managing the PowerPoint Environment
1.1. Adjust views

View: Switch Windows

2. Try This: Switch Windows
There are two slide shows open.
Go to **View ->Switch Windows.**

What Do You See? The first presentation, Hats Off to Spring, is now in front.
No surprises here. Keep going...

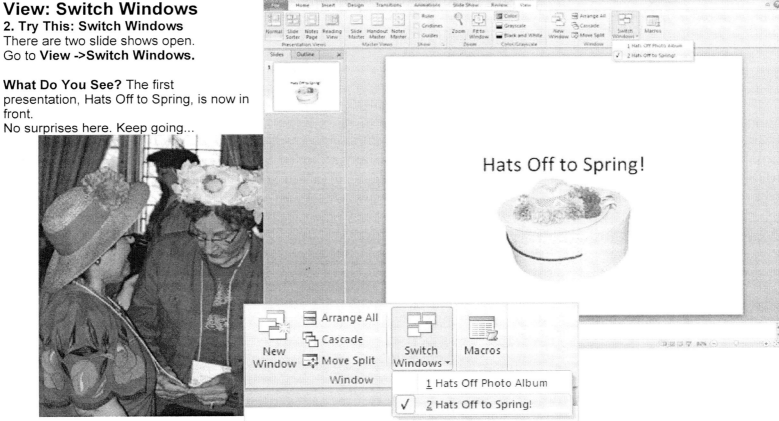

Exam 77-883: Microsoft PowerPoint 2010
1. Managing the PowerPoint Environment
1.1. Adjust views: Switch Windows

View: Arrange All

When you **Switch** Windows, you are choosing one presentation over another. The other shows will be hidden behind it. You can also **Arrange All** to see more than one slide show at a time.

3. Try it: Arrange All of the Windows
Go to **View ->Window->Arrange All**.

What Do You See? The two slide shows are displayed side by side.

What Else Do You See? The Ribbons have abbreviated groups. The Windows group has been reduced to a single icon.

Keep going...

View ->Window->Arrange All

Exam 77-883: Microsoft PowerPoint 2010
1. Managing the PowerPoint Environment
1.1. Adjust views: Arrange All Windows

View: Cascade

4. Try it: Use the Cascade View
There are two slide shows open.
Go to **View ->Window->Cascade.**

What Do You See? The **Cascade** View lets you see all of the presentations, each in their own PowerPoint Window. You can click on any presentation to bring it to the front so that you can edit it.

Keep going...

View ->Window->Cascade

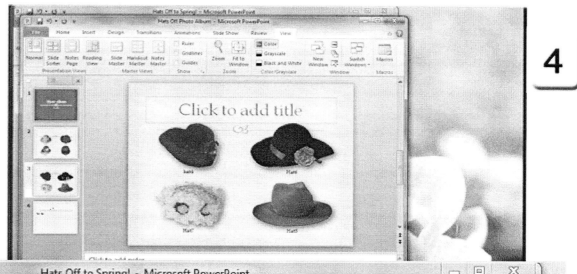

Exam 77-883: Microsoft PowerPoint 2010
1. Managing the PowerPoint Environment
1.2. Manipulate the PowerPoint window: Work with Multiple Presentation Windows Simulataneously

View: Zoom

The Computer Mama sez: the older you get the more you appreciate the **Zoom** control. Zoom magnifies your work.

5. Try it: Zoom into a Presentation
Either slide show is open and on top.
Go to **View ->Zoom->Zoom.**

What Do You See? There are several built-in magnifications. You can type your own **Percent** if you wish.

Try This, Too: Fit to Window
Go to **View ->Zoom->Fit to Window**

What Do You See, Now? Your slide show will be resized to fit the Window.

Look Again: Zoom changes the View. It does not resize the PowerPoint Window.

Keep going...

Exam 77-883: Microsoft PowerPoint 2010
1. Managing the PowerPoint Environment
1.1. Adjust views: Zoom!

View: Color/Grayscale

There are three more options for adjusting the View: **Color, Grayscale** (as if it is a Xerox copy) and **Black and White**.

Before You Begin: Make both slide shows full screen, please. The Zoom should be set to Fit on Screen.

6. Try it: Change the View to Grayscale
Select either presentation.
Go to **View ->Color/Grayscale**.
Select: **Grayscale**.

What Do You See? All of the slides will be formatted. PowerPoint has a Grayscale Ribbon. The Grayscale formatting can be applied to each picture separately as well.

Please return **Back to Color View**.
Save, Save, Save.

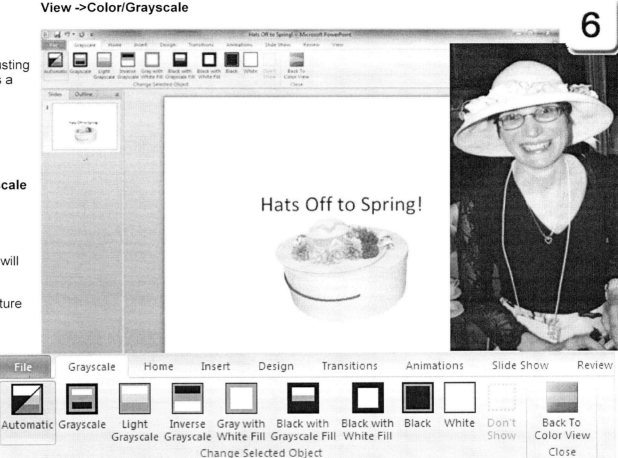

Exam 77-883: Microsoft PowerPoint 2010
1. Managing the PowerPoint Environment
1.1. Adjust views: Color/Grayscale

Combining Slide Shows

Say you wanted to combine the three "Spring" presentations into one show. Here are some thoughts to consider:

Can you choose some, or all of the slides in another presentation?

Will the new slides match the rest of the slide show?

Can you create Sections and format the Themes differently?

1. Try it: Edit the Presentation
Open the presentation: Hats Off to Spring.pptx

Go to **Design ->Theme**.
Select: Clarity.
Go to **Design ->Theme->Colors**.
Select: Opulent.

Keep going...

Design ->Theme

Exam 77-883: Microsoft PowerPoint 2010
2. Creating a Slide Presentation
2.4. Format slides: Modify Themes

New Slide: Reuse Slides

Here are the steps to add slides from a different presentation. This example will use a slide show that was created in an earlier lesson. You can download a copy if you wish.

1. Try it: Reuse Slides
The Presentation is open.
Go to **Home ->Slides->New Slide.**
Click on **Reuse Slides...**

Keep going...

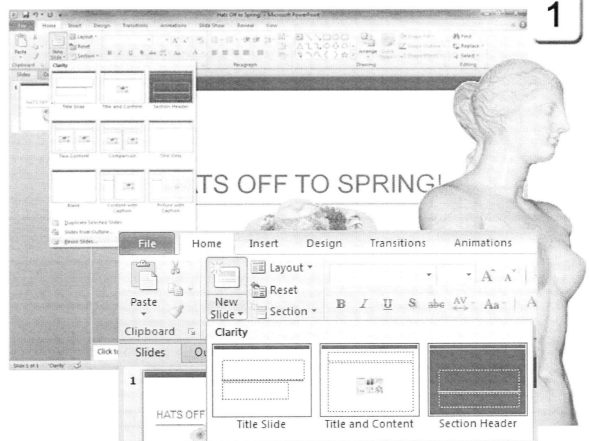

Exam 77-883: Microsoft PowerPoint 2010
2. Creating a Slide Presentation
2.3. Add and remove slides: Reuse slides

Home ->Slides->New Slide->Reuse Slides

Reuse Slides:
2. Try it: Review the Options
There are several ways to copy slides into your presentation, including:

Insert slide from: This option lets you Browse for your slide show.

Open a Slide Library: This option lets you create a library of the slides you may want to use in many presentations.

Open a PowerPoint File: This option is similar to Insert slide from.

Keep going...

Exam 77-883: Microsoft PowerPoint 2010
2. Creating a Slide Presentation
2.3. Add and remove slides: Reuse slides

Reuse Slides: From File

3. Try it: Insert Slides From File
Go to **Insert Slides From...**
Browse for a presentation.
Select: Song of Solomon.
Click **OK** to open the presentation.

Keep going...

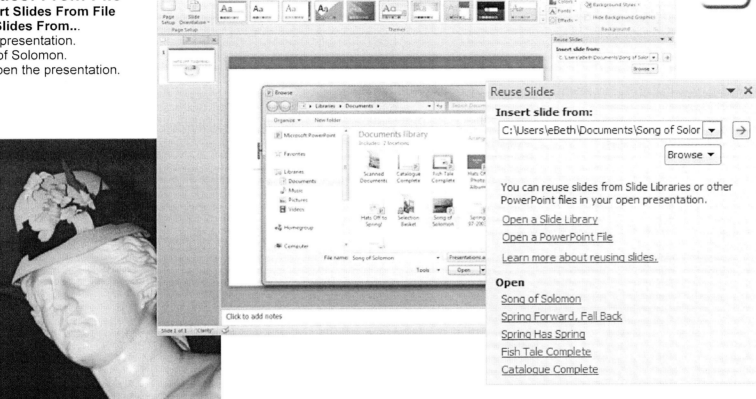

Exam 77-883: Microsoft PowerPoint 2010
2. Creating a Slide Presentation
2.3. Add and remove slides: Reuse slides

Reuse Slides: Add a Slide

All four slides from the Song of Solomon presentation are displayed on the right in the Task Pane.

4. Try it: Select the Slides
Go to the **Reuse Slides** Task Pane.
Click on Slide 4 of Song of Solomon.

What Do You See? Slide 4 was added to your presentation. The new slide inherited the same **Theme** and **Theme Color** as the original show, Hats Off to Spring.

What Else Do You See? By default, PowerPoint formats the new slides so that they will match.

Please look at the bottom of the **Reuse Slides** Task Pane. You can also select **Keep Source formatting** if you wish.

☐ Keep source formatting

So far, so good.

Exam 77-883: Microsoft PowerPoint 2010
2. Creating a Slide Presentation
2.3. Add and remove slides: Reuse slides

Add a Section

Say you wanted to combine several slide shows together. Working with many, many slides can get confusing. Microsoft PowerPoint uses **Sections** to organize the slides in your presentation. The Sections also help you navigate long slide shows.

Before You Begin: Slide 2 is selected.
Place your cursor under Slide 2.
Look for a **black line** like this:

1. Try it: Insert a Section
Go to **Home->Slides->Section**.
Click on **Add Section.**

What Do You See? There should be a new, **Untitled Section** under Slide 2.
Keep going...

Exam 77-883: Microsoft PowerPoint 2010
2. Creating a Slide Presentation
2.4. Format slides: Add Sections

Rename the New Section

2. Try it: Rename the Section
Right-Click **Untitled Section**.
Click on **Rename Section**.
Type the Name: Section 2.
Click **Rename**.

Keep going...

Memo to Self: The same option can be found on the **Home** Ribbon:
Home ->Slides->Section.
Click on **Rename Section.**

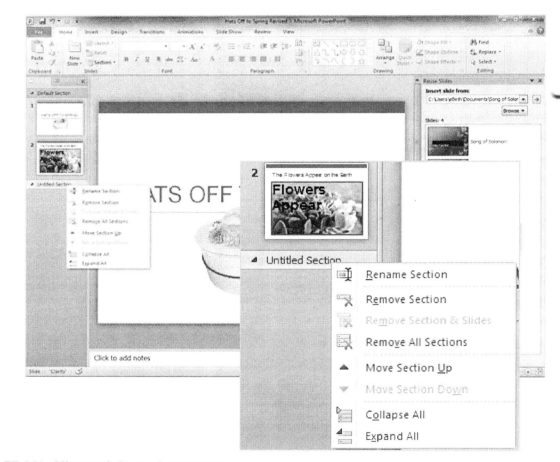

Exam 77-883: Microsoft PowerPoint 2010
2. Creating a Slide Presentation
2.4. Format slides: Rename Sections

Add to the New Section

Please add 2 slides to Section 2. The new slides should keep the same formatting as Song of Solomon, the Source.

3. Try This: Add Slides to Section 2.
Place your cursor under Section 2.
The **Reuse Slides** Task Pane is open.
Select: Slide 3 and Slide 4.
Check: Keep source formatting.

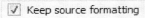

What Do You See? The new slides should be added to Section 2. The slides should keep the Theme and colors they had in the Source presentation.

Keep going...

Memo to Self: When you add slides out of order that is called **non-contiguous.**

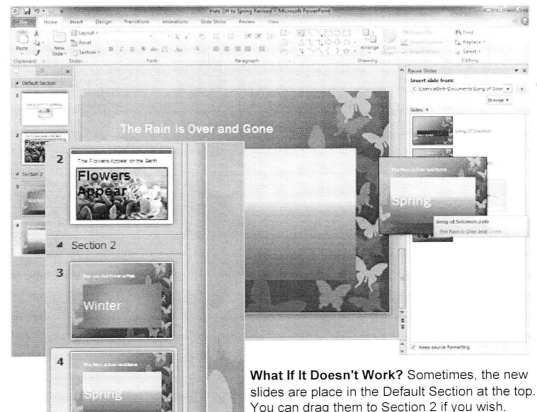

What If It Doesn't Work? Sometimes, the new slides are place in the Default Section at the top. You can drag them to Section 2 if you wish.

Exam 77-883: Microsoft PowerPoint 2010
2. Creating a Slide Presentation
2.3. Add and remove slides: Add Non-contiguous Slides in a Presentation

Working with Sections

4. Try it: Use Sections
Click on Section 2.
Section 2, and all of its slides, should be
highlighted and selected.

Right Click Section 2.
The **Section** options include:
Rename Section
Remove Section
Remove Section & Slides
Remove All Sections
Move Section Up
Move Section Down
Collapse All
Expand All

OK, look but don't touch. Let's move on...

Memo to Self: You can use the Sections
to move or delete multiple slides
simultaneously.

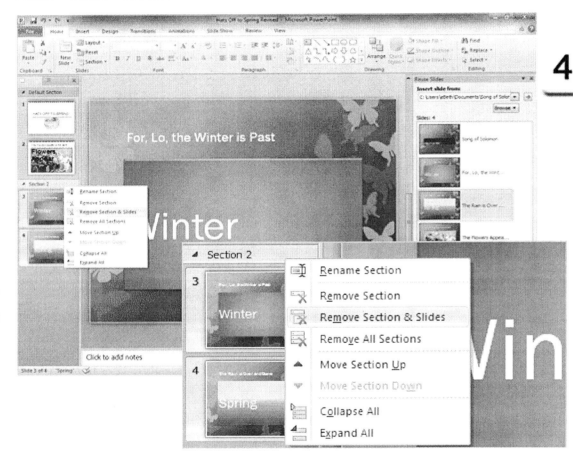

Exam 77-883: Microsoft PowerPoint 2010
2. Creating a Slide Presentation
 2.3. Add and remove slides: Use Sections to Remove Multiple Slides

Format a Section

Here's a task: can you choose a Section and format the Theme?

5. Try it: Format a Section.
Section 2 and all of its slides are selected.

Go to **Design ->Theme.**
Select: Austin.

What Do You See? The slides in Section 2 were formatted with the new Theme. The slides in the other Section did not change.

How Big Can You Make a Slide Show? PowerPoint can handle big presentations. However, you might want to consider your audience and how long they want to sit.

The Computer Mama Sez: I will ALWAYS remember the day I had to endure a presentation with over 300 slides. Each slide had a chapter story on it that the presenter read out loud, word for word.
(!!!)

Design ->Theme

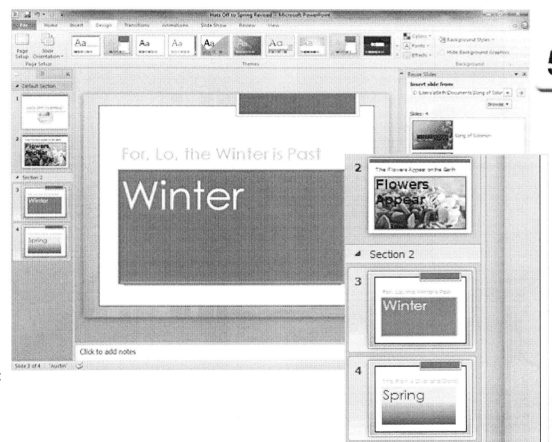

Exam 77-883: Microsoft PowerPoint 2010
2. Creating a Slide Presentation
2.4. Format slides: Format Sections

A Different View

There is another benefit to working with Sections that becomes more apparent when you choose a different **View**: the **Slide Sorter**.

Try it: Find the Slide Sorter
Go to **View ->Presentation Views**.
Click on **Slide Sorter**.

What Do You See? The Normal View uses a Text Outline. The Slide Sorter displays the slides as images for those of us who think in pictures.

Memo to Self: Look at the bottom of PowerPoint Window at the Status Bar. In the right corner are little 'quick view' buttons. The options include: Normal, Slide Sorter, Reading View, and Slide Show. There is a slider to change the Zoom.

View ->Presentation Views->Slide Sorter

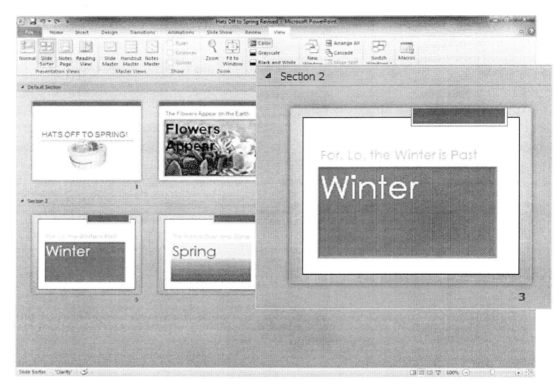

Exam 77-883: Microsoft PowerPoint 2010
1. Managing the PowerPoint Environment
1.1. Adjust views: Change the View with the Ribbon or the Status Bar

Slide Sorter: Sections

Let's add a new Section in the Slide Sorter View. Here are the steps.

1. Try it: Create a New Section
Place your cursor after Slide 4 in Section 2.
Go to **Home->Slides->Section.**
Click on **Add Section.**
Right Click->Rename.
Type the name: Section 3.

▷ Section 3 (0 slides)

2. Try This: Reuse Slides
Go to **Home ->Slides->New Slide.**
Click on **Reuse Slides...**
Go to **Insert slide from:**
Browse for a presentation.
Select: Spring Forward Fall Back.pptx.

3. Try This, Too: Insert All of the Slides
Right Click any slide in the Reuse Slide pane.
Select: **Insert All Slides.**

Keep going...

View ->Presentation Views->Slide Sorter

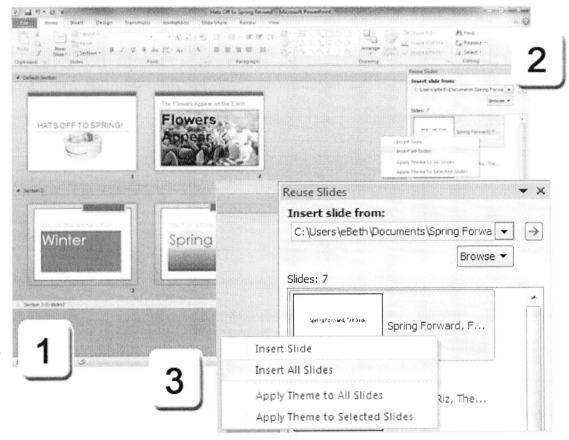

Exam 77-883: Microsoft PowerPoint 2010
2. Creating a Slide Presentation
2.4. Format slides: Format Sections

Slide Sorter: Sections

4. What Do You See? The new slides added to Section 3 may inherit the Theme from the Section 2. Again, if the new slides end up in Section 2, you can drag them down to Section 3.

Save, Save, Save.
File Name: Hats Off to Spring Revised..

View ->Slide Sorter

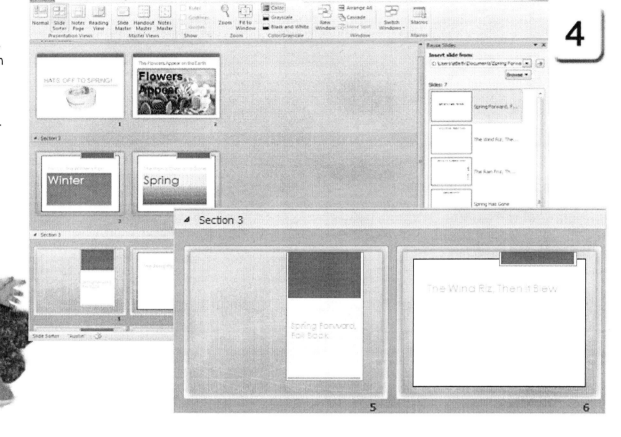

Creating a Slide Library

A **Slide Library** is a shared folder for your slides. Many presentations can the use the same slides. One example would be the Company Name slide that lists everyone in the firm or working on this project.

The Slide Library keeps the latest versions of these slides. It is updated automatically and keeps a record of any changes made to the slide. Say, Mary Contrary got married and became Mary O'Hara.

1. Try it: Create a Slide Library
Open a sample presentation:
Hat's Off Photo Album.pptx.

Keep going...

File ->Open

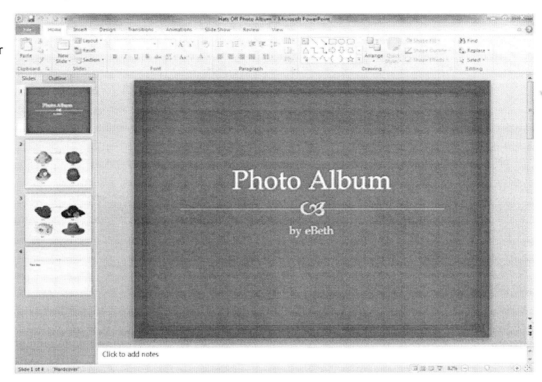

Exam 77-883: Microsoft PowerPoint 2010
2. Creating a Slide Presentation
2.3. Add and remove slides: Reuse Slides from a Slide Library

Publish a Presentation

Before you can create a **Slide Library**, you need to **Publish the Slides** in your presentations. Microsoft PowerPoint uses the Backstage to Save and Send.

2. Try it: Publish Slides
The sample presentation is open.
Go to **File ->Save & Send.**
Click on **Publish Slides**.

Keep going...

Memo to Self: The example on these pages demonstrates how to create a personal Slide Library that manages your slides. In a business or school, the folder would be shared on a server that everyone can access.

File ->Save & Send->Publish Slides

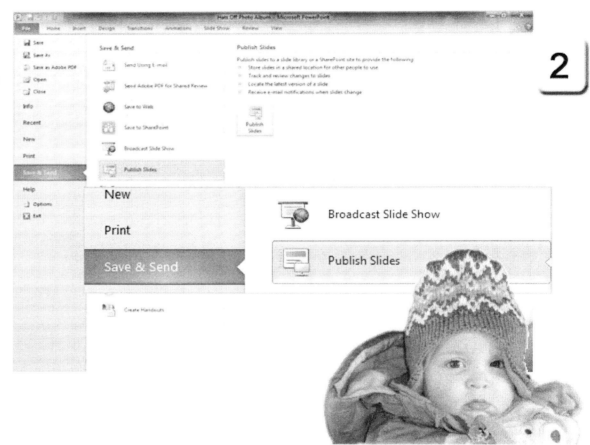

Exam 77-883: Microsoft PowerPoint 2010
2. Creating a Slide Presentation
2.3. Add and remove slides: Reuse Slides from a Slide Library

Publish Slides: Options

3. Try it: Select the Slides
You can select any or all of the slides in this presentation if you wish.

4. Try This, Too: Create a Folder
Click on Browse.
By default you will be taken to:
PowerPoint->My Slide Libraries.

Click on **New Folder** at the top of the Browse Window.
Name the New Folder: Spring Slides

5. And Try This: Publish the Slides
Click **Publish**.

Please turn the page...

File ->Save & Send->Publish Slides

Exam 77-883: Microsoft PowerPoint 2010
2. Creating a Slide Presentation
2.3. Add and remove slides: Reuse Slides from a Slide Library

Home ->Slides->New Slide->Reuse Slides

Browse the Slide Library

1. Try it: Open a Slide Library
Open the presentation:
Hats Off to Spring Revised.

Go to **Home ->Slides->New Slide.**
Click on **Reuse Slides.**
Go to **Browse->Browse Slide Library**.

Keep going...

Exam 77-883: Microsoft PowerPoint 2010
2. Creating a Slide Presentation
2.3. Add and remove slides: Reuse Slides from a Slide Library

Use the Slide Library

2. Try it: Reuse Slides from a Library
Each slide that was saved to the Library folder can be opened in the Slides task pane and added to your presentation.

The Computer Mama sez: It may be difficult to Publish and Open a Slide Library. The permissions on the default folder may not allow you to save or see the files that were published. Hmmm.

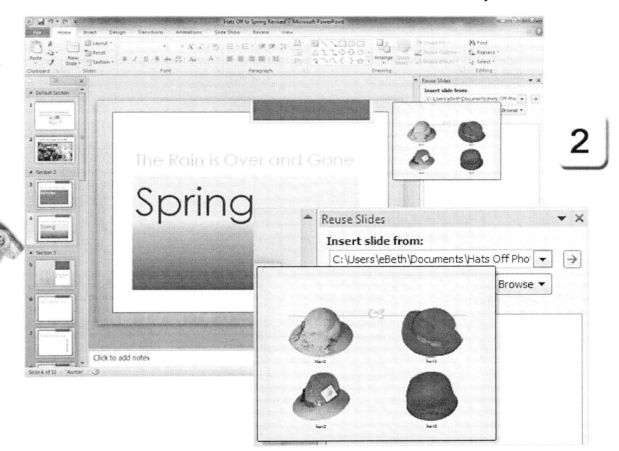

Exam 77-883: Microsoft PowerPoint 2010
2. Creating a Slide Presentation
2.3. Add and remove slides: Reuse Slides from a Slide Library

Summary

This lesson began with a discussion about the different **Views** in PowerPoint. We looked at how to work effectively when two or more presentations are open.

We also reviewed the options for adding slides from other presentations and placing them in different Sections.

This concludes the *Beginning Guide to Microsoft PowerPoint*. If you've come this far, please join us for Animation and Action in the *Advanced Guide to Microsoft PowerPoint*.

You done real good.

Extra for Experts

There are several useful options that just beg to be taught. The following pages have a couple of Extras for Experts.

The cool part of working with PowerPoint is how easy it is to change your mind. You can choose a shape and make it the default instead of accepting the built in standard. You can also convert one object into another.

1. Try it: Create a New Presentation:
Open the presentation:
Extra for Experts.pptx.
This slide show has four slides.

Keep going...

File ->Open

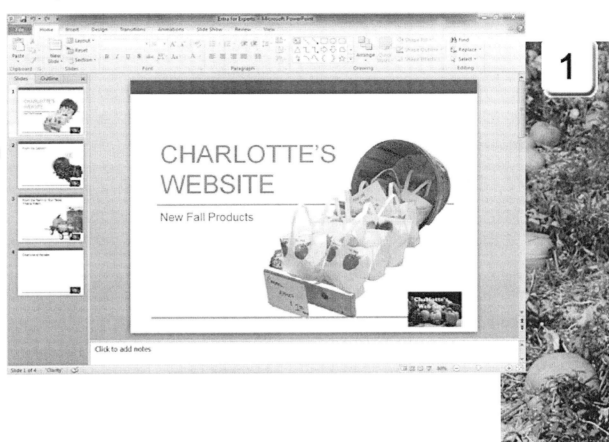

Format the Text Box

2. Try it: Create and Format the Text Box
Select to Slide 2: From the Garden.
Go to **Insert ->Text->Text Box.**
Draw a Text Box.

Try This, Too: Enter the Sample Text
Select the Text Box and type the following:
New fruits
New veggies
New desserts

And Try This: Format the Text Box
Select the Text Box.
Go to **Drawing Tools->Format->Shape Styles**.
Choose a **Style**: Intense Effect: Dark Red, Accent 1.

Go to **Drawing Tools->Format->Shape Styles.**
Go to **Shape Effects->Bevel**.
Choose a **Bevel Effect**: Circle.

Go to **Drawing Tools->Format->Shape Styles.**
Go to **Shape Effects->Shadow.**
Choose a **Shadow Effect**: Perspective Below.

Keep going...

Exam 77-883: Microsoft PowerPoint 2010
2. Creating a Slide Presentation
2.6. Format text boxes.: Set the current Text Box as the default

Text Box: Set as Default

Say you wanted all of the new Text Boxes in this presentation to be formatted the same. This is really easy.

3. Try it: Set Current Text Box as Default
Right-click the red Text Box.
Select **Set as Default.**

Now, whenever you create a new Text Box, it will be formatted red with a bevel and a drop shadow. This is faster than using the Format Painter, although that would work as well.

Very good. Keep going...

Insert ->Text->Text Box

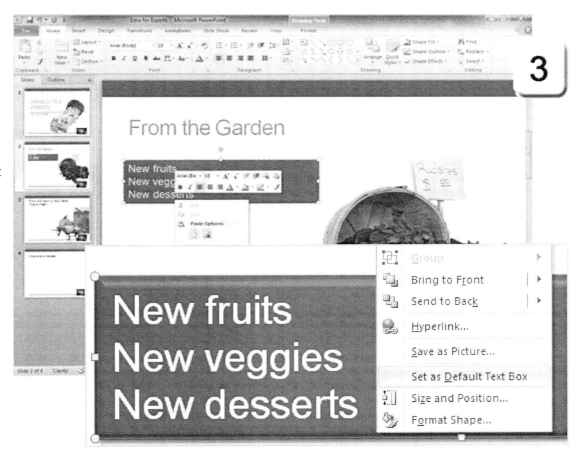

Exam 77-883: Microsoft PowerPoint 2010
2. Creating a Slide Presentation
2.6. Format text boxes.: Set the current Text Box as the default

Insert ->Illustrations->Shapes

Text Boxes are Shapes

A Text Box is just a Shape. You can format a Shape, color it red, add bevel and shadow Effects, and make that the default formatting for new Shapes as well.

4. Try it: Set Current Text Box as Default
Select to Slide 2: From the Garden.
Go to **Insert ->Illustrations->Shapes**.
Select a Shape: **Arrow Right**.

And Try This: Format the Shape
Select the Shape.
Go to **Drawing Tools->Format->Shape Styles**.
Choose a **Style**: Intense Effect: Dark Red, Accent 1.

Go to **Shape Effects->Bevel**.
Choose a Bevel Effect: Circle.

Go to **Shape Effects->Shadow**.
Choose a Shadow Effect: Perspective Below.

Keep going...

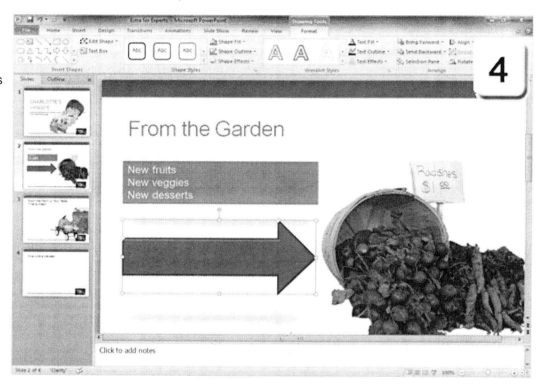

Exam 77-883: Microsoft PowerPoint 2010
3. Working with Graphical and Multimedia Elements
3.3. Modify WordArt and shapes: Set Current Shape as the Default

Shape: Set as Default

Now that the Shape is formatted, go ahead and make this the default.

5. Try it: Set Current Shape as Default
Right-click the red Shape.
Select: **Set as Default**.

So, whenever you create a new Shape, whether it is a rectangle, an arrow or a heart, it will be formatted red with a bevel and a drop shadow.

Keep going...

Exam 77-883: Microsoft PowerPoint 2010
3. Working with Graphical and Multimedia Elements
3.3. Modify WordArt and shapes: Set Current Shape as the Default

Change the Shape of a Text Box

Say you wanted a different Shape for the Text Box. Here are the steps.

6. Try it: Change the Shape of a Text Box
Select the Text Box on Slide 2.
Go to **Drawing Tools ->Format ->Insert Shape.**
Go to **Edit Shape->Change Shape**
Select a new Shape: Explosion1.

Keep going...

Drawing Tools ->Format ->Insert Shape->Edit Shape->Change Shape

6

Exam 77-883: Microsoft PowerPoint 2010
2. Creating a Slide Presentation
2.6. Format text boxes: Change the Shape of a Text Box

Convert Text to SmartArt

7. Try it: Convert Text to SmartArt

Go to Slide 3 and enter the following text:
Fruits
Veggies
Desserts

Select the bulleted list.
Go to **Home ->Paragraph.**
Click on **Convert to SmartArt Graphic.**
Select a Graphic: **Chevron List**.

Keep going, this looks cool...

Home ->Paragraph->Convert to SmartArt Graphic

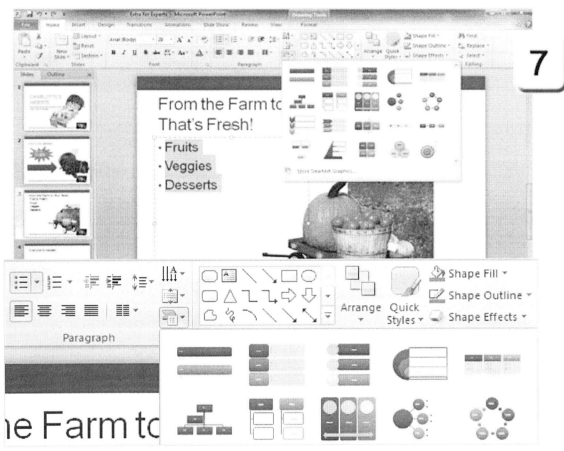

Exam 77-883: Microsoft PowerPoint 2010
2. Creating a Slide Presentation
2.5. Enter and format text: Convert Text to SmartArt

Convert Text to SmartArt

8. What Do You See? You should see a new SmartArt graphic on Slide 3. The SmartArt Tools should be available.

When you select one of the Shapes in the SmartArt graphic, the Shape Styles on the Format Ribbon should also become available.

Keep going...one more smart conversion.

SmartArt Tools ->Design

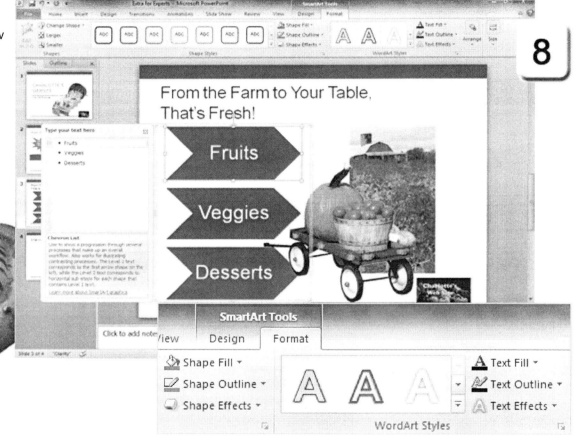

Exam 77-883: Microsoft PowerPoint 2010
2. Creating a Slide Presentation
2.5. Enter and format text: Convert Text to SmartArt

Convert WordArt to SmartArt
Say you had a WordArt graphic and wanted something more dynamic. Please try this.

9. Try it: Create a New WordArt Graphic
Go to Slide 4: Charlotte's Website.
Go to **Insert ->Illustrations->SmartArt.**
Enter the following Text:
Quality
Quantity
Fresh!

Try This, Too: Convert WordArt to SmartArt
 Select the WordArt.
Go to **Home->Paragraph**.
Click on **Convert to SmartArt**.
Select the SmartArt: Continuous Block.

Keep going...

Insert ->Illustrations->SmartArt

Exam 77-883: Microsoft PowerPoint 2010
3. Working with Graphical and Multimedia Elements
3.3. Modify WordArt and shapes: Convert WordArt to SmartArt

Smart, Very Smart

What Do You See? The WordArt was converted into SmartArt. The SmartArt Tools--Design and Format--should be available.

SmartArt is a great tool for creating rich graphics. We've looked at the SmartArt Styles and Formatting in previous lessons.

Please take a few more minutes to look at an advanced Paragraph option and the Slide Setup. Keep going...

Exam 77-883: Microsoft PowerPoint 2010
3. Working with Graphical and Multimedia Elements
3.3. Modify WordArt and shapes: Convert WordArt to SmartArt

Just One More...

By default, a slide is 6x9 with a Text Box in the middle formatted for bulleted lists. The following pages show two unusual options that you can consider: changing the Slide Orientation and formatting the Text Box for two columns.

1. Try it: Create a New Slide
Slide 4 is selected.
Go to **Home ->Slides->New Slide.**
Select: Title and Content

Keep going...

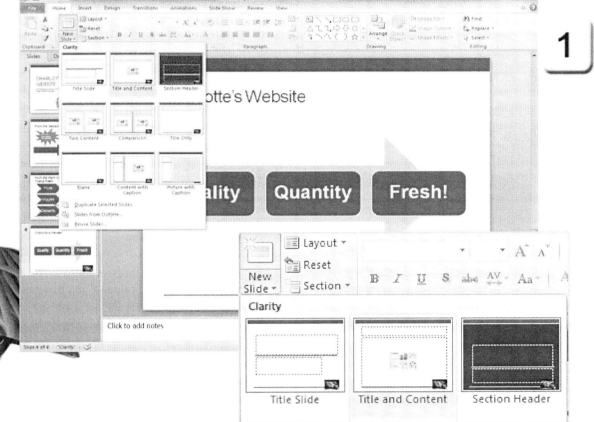

Exam 77-883: Microsoft PowerPoint 2010
2. Creating a Slide Presentation
2.6. Format text boxes: Create Columns in a Text Box

Change the Page Set Up

Slide size and orientation can be found on the Design Ribbon, next to the Themes.

2. Try it: Change the Page Setup
Go to **Design ->Page Setup.**
Click on **Page Setup**

Try This, as well: Edit the Page Setup
Slides sized for: **Custom**
Width: 8 inches
Height: 10 inches
Slide **Orientation**: **Portrait**

Click **OK**. Keep going, please...

Design ->Page Setup->Page Setup

Exam 77-883: Microsoft PowerPoint 2010
2. Creating a Slide Presentation
2.2. Apply slide size and orientation settings: Setup a Custom Size

Page Setup: Slide Orientation

3. Try it: Review the Page Setup

All of the slides in the presentation have a new size and orientation. Like Themes, Page Setup is applied to the whole show.

Where are we going here....?

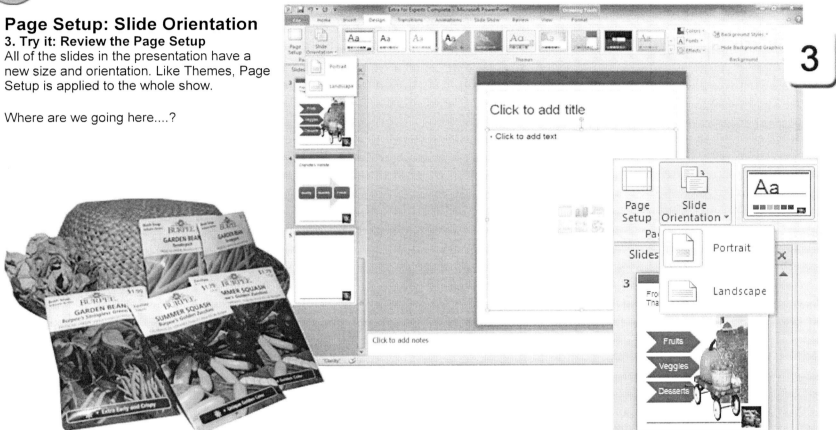

Exam 77-883: Microsoft PowerPoint 2010
2. Creating a Slide Presentation
2.2. Apply slide size and orientation settings: Change the Orientation

Make Columns in a Text Box
Before You Begin: Add the sample text
Title: New Products
Text Box: Add Item 1-Item 8 as shown.

4. Try it: Format the Columns
Select the sample test: Item 1-Item 8.
Go to **Design ->Page Setup->Columns**
Select: Two Columns.

What Did You See? Nothing, not yet.

Still wondering where this is going?
Turn the page...

Design ->Page Setup->Columns

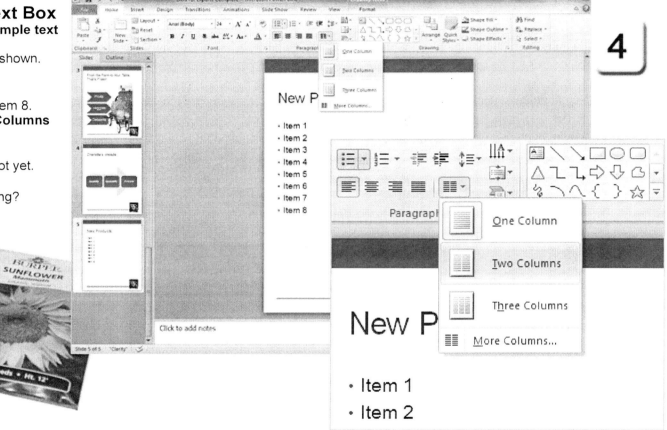

Exam 77-883: Microsoft PowerPoint 2010
2. Creating a Slide Presentation
2.6. Format text boxes: Create Columns in a Text Box

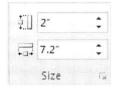

Change the Size of a Text Box

4. Try it: Format the Text Box Size
Select the Text Box on Slide 5.
Go to **Drawing Tools ->Size->Height**
Type: 2.

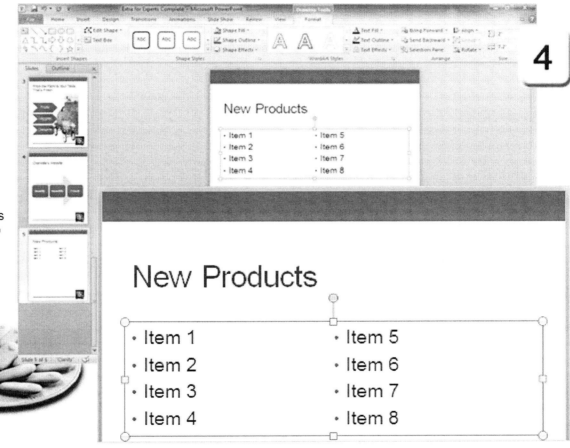

What Did You See? When the Text Box was resized, the bulleted list repaginated into two even columns.

OK, that worked. **Save** your presentation.
Allez, Allez In Free! You done real good.

Exam 77-883: Microsoft PowerPoint 2010
2. Creating a Slide Presentation
2.6. Format text boxes: Change the Size

Practice Activities

Lesson 7: Photo Albums and Views

Try This: Do the following steps

1. Open a new blank presentation.
2. Insert a photo album. Add the four crane sample pictures found online.
   a. Rotate picture crane 2 counter clockwise so the birds are right-side up
   b. Adjust the brightness on crane 4 until the picture is no longer washed out
   c. Reorder the picture so that Crane 4 is the first picture
3. Save the photo album presentation as Birds1.
4. Open the sample presentation Sandhill Cranes
5. Apply the Theme Spring (or a theme of your choice.)
6. Reuse the slides from the Birds 1 photo album presentation. Sort the photo slides in an order that makes sense to you.
7. Save this file as Sandhill Cranes with Photos
8. Open another new blank slide show. Add the title: More Facts on Sandhill Cranes
   a. Add each of the facts on its own slide
      i. Adults are gray
      ii. They have a red forehead and a dark bill
      iii. Wingspan is 5-7 ft
      iv They fly south for the winter
   b. Apply the Theme Adjacency.
   c. Save this file as More Sandhill Facts. Close this file.
9. Return to the Sandhill Cranes with Photos presentation.
   a. Add a section break after the last slide.
   b. Reuse the slides from More Sandhill Facts. Insert the slides in Section 2 and Keep Source Formatting.
10. Rename Section 2 as More Facts
11. Change the Theme in Section 1 of the Sandhill Cranes with Photos presentation to be Solstice
12. Add a picture of your choice to each slide of the More Facts Section.
13. Change the entire presentation to be Grayscale
14. Save the file as Beginning PowerPoint Practice Activity 6.

Test Yourself

1. What Ribbon has the command for adding a Photo Album?
a. Insert
b. Home
c. New
d. Design
Tip: Beginning PowerPoint, page 195

2. Which are Picture Album options? (Give all correct answers)
a. Captions below All pictures
b. All pictures black and white
Tip: Beginning PowerPoint, page 197

3. You can adjust individual pictures in a PowerPoint Photo Album.
a. True
b. False
Tip: Beginning PowerPoint, page 198

4. Which are adjustments you can make in a PowerPoint Photo Album

(Give all correct answers)
a. Rotation left or right
b. Contrast increase or decrease
c. Brightness increase or decrease
Tip: Beginning PowerPoint, page 198

5. The option to add captions is not available until you choose a Layout that includes text.
a. True
b. False
Tip: Beginning PowerPoint, page 200

6. Which is NOT a group on the View Ribbon?
a. Presentation Views
b. Page Layout
c. Zoom
d. Window
Tip: Beginning PowerPoint, page 204

7. Which are Window View commands? (Give all correct answers)
a. Switch windows
b. Arrange all
c. Cascade
Tip: Beginning PowerPoint, page 205

8. Zoom resizes the PowerPoint window.
a. True
b. False
Tip: Beginning PowerPoint, page 208

9. Which is the command to reuse slides
a. Insert--> New Slide--> Reuse Slide
b. Home--> Slides--> New Slide--> Reuse Slide
c. Home--> Reuse Slide
Tip: Beginning PowerPoint, page 211

10. Which of the following is true about inserting slides from an old presentation into a new presentation? (Give all correct answers)
a. The inserted slides inherit the new presentations Theme by default
b. The inserted slides can be set to Keep Source formatting
Tip: Beginning PowerPoint, page 214

Beginning PowerPoint Skill Test

Please do the following steps:
1. Open a new blank presentation.
2. Add the Title: Robert Frost
3. Add the following facts about Robert Frost
   Born in 1874
   Died in 1963
   American Poet
   Won the Pulitzer Prize 4 times
   More than any other poet in history

4. Change the bullet points to a different shape.
5. Demote Died in 1863 one list level.
6. Demote More than any other poet in history one list level
7. Format the font to a different color and font of your choice
8. Format the line spacing to be 2.0
9. Add a new slide.
   a. Change the layout to Title Only.
   Add the following quote as the Title:
   I have never started a poem yet whose end I knew.
   Writing a poem is discovering.
   b. Add the subtitle: Robert Frost on writing
   c. Format the subtitle to be aligned left.
   d. Format the Text Box with a Style of your choice
10. Apply the Theme Newsprint.
11. Add a picture of your choice on slide 2.
    Apply a Picture Style of your choice.

12. Add a picture of your choice on slide 3.
a. Apply an Artistic Effect of your choice.
b. Crop the picture to a shape of your choice.
13. Add a new slide. Add the following quote to the content area:
Poetry is what gets lost in translation.
a. Format the Text Direction as Rotate 270 degrees.
b. Format the text box with a Gradient Fill of your choice
c. Add a picture of your choice.
d. Apply a Reflection picture effect of your choice.
14. Add a new slide. Insert Smart Art Organizational Chart
a. At the top, add the name Robert Frost
b. In the second box down add the text American Poet
c. Add the text Born 1873 and demote it one list level lower than American Poet
d. Add the following poem titles at the bottom level: A Patch of Old Snow, Stopping by the Woods, Mending Wall, and Nothing Gold Can Stay
e. Apply a Smart Art Style and color set of your choice
f. Change the Robert Frost shape to a different color than the rest of your Smart Art
g. Change the American Poet shape to be an oval shape.
15. Add a new section. Rename Section 2 as Poem
16. Reuse slides from the Stopping by the Woods presentation. Insert the first two slides and KEEP source formatting.
17. Save this file as Your Name Beginning PowerPoint Skill Test.

Beginning Microsoft PowerPoint 2010: Index
Microsoft Office Specialist (MOS): Exam 77-883 for PowerPoint 2010

Beginning Microsoft PowerPoint 2010: Glossary
Microsoft Office Specialist (MOS): Exam 77-883 for PowerPoint 2010

Alignment-- how text is lined up on a slide, relative to the edges. Can be left, right, centered, top or bottom, pg.75

Case-- term that refers to whether the text is capitalized, or not, pg.36

Character spacing-- the amount of space between letters, aka kerning, pg.35

Clipboard-- a helper application that stores text or pictures to be pasted. Activated with use of the cut or copy commands, pg.41

Compress (picture)-- reduces the size of a picture's storage size, but not its visible size, pg.148

Crop marks-- marks similar to handles that are used to show and resize the cropped areas of a picture, pg.140

Crop-- trims the edges of the picture, pg.140

File type-- refers to the type of coding used in a file, defining what program(s) will open the file and how the program treats the contents. pg.49

Gradient Fill-- method for creating a gradual change in the intensity of color, pg.92

Handles-- small icons on the corner and sides of objects, such as pictures, shapes or text boxes, in an Office document or file to show where the edges of the object are. Can be used to resize an object, pg.134

Leading (see also line spacing)-- Amount of space between lines of text, such as double-spaced with one blank line between lines of text, pg.73

Line spacing (see also leading)-- amount of space between lines of text, such as double-spaced with one blank line between lines of text. pg.73

Live Preview-- allows the user to see possible changes to text, images, shapes, etc. before applying those changes, pg.108

Multi-level list-- organizes your information into topics and sub-topics, pg.71

Outline-- a general overview of a topic, highlighting main points. In PowerPoint, an Outline is used to organize information either on slides or, using Outline View, for the entire presentation, pg.60

Photo Album-- a special type of PowerPoint presentation that displays photos similar to a book of photos. Includes options for captions and editing, pg. 194

Placeholder-- a set of icons on a slide that both holds the place of future content and allows quick access to adding content to that textbox, pg. 130

Section-- a division in a presentation, used to organize content, pg.215

Shape-- a text box with custom formatting. Shapes are modified with the Drawing Tools, pg.85

Slide library-- shared folder for slides. Allows ease in reusing common slides, pg.212

Slide Sorter-- shows thumbnail images of the slides and provides a visual outline of the presentation, pg.220

Slides-- individual 'pages' used in a PowerPoint presentation, pg. 29

SmartArt-- dynamic, graphics, charts and diagrams, pg.170

Styles--collection of preset formatting to be applied to text or objects. pg.91

Theme-- when applied, formats text, paragraph, layout and color palette, pg.111

Title slide-- a slide that is formatted differently than the others, used like a book cover to introduce a new topic, pg.30